READING OTHERWAYS

For Jac

with thanks for all

I learn

Lissa

LISSA PAUL

Reading Otherways

THE THIMBLE PRESS

My thanks
to the librarians at the Osborne Collection of Early Children's Books,
Toronto, and the Toronto Public Library for all their patient help;
the illustrations on pages 21 and 27 are reproduced
from books held in the Osborne Collection;
to Karma Dyenka, Peter Gorham, Yu Ming Ye
Zinpai Zangmo and Mary Jo Marsden
who gave me permission to tell their stories;
to Roger Simon, for permission to reproduce the mural, page 19;
to Nina Bawden and Ted Hughes for permision to quote from their letters.
LISSA PAUL

Illustrations
Page 26: *The Fairy Tales of Charles Perrault* illustrations © Martin Ware 1977
Victor Gollancz, London, 1977
Page 35: *Hansel and Gretel* © Anthony Browne 1981
Julia MacRae Books, London, 1981
Page 38: *The Little Mermaid* © 1983 Laszlo Gal &
Margaret Crawford Maloney, Methuen Publications, Canada, 1983

Reading Otherways comes from The Thimble Press,
publishers since January 1970 of the thrice-yearly journal
Signal Approaches to Children's Books
and other writings on literature and literacy.

First published 1998 by
THE THIMBLE PRESS
Lockwood, Station Road, Woodchester
Stroud, Glos. GL5 5EQ
0145387 3716 phone   0145387 8599 fax

British Library Cataloguing-in-Publication Data
A catalogue record for this book is available from the
British Library

Printed in Great Britain
by Short Run Press, Exeter

ISBN 0 903355 46 9

CONTENTS

1. TOWARDS A BEGINNING 7
Penetrating the darkness 8
Reading differently 15
The problem with looking through feminist eyes . . . 17

2. WHAT THE TALES TELL 23
Other ways of reading 31
Now you see it . . . 36

3. READING *LITTLE WOMEN* 40
The Ministering Angel 42
Is *Little Women* still worth reading? 50

4. *CARRIE'S WAR*: READING FEMINIST CHANGES 56
Outside the margins 58
Reading *Carrie's War* 61
Reading the power structures 63
The Witch and the Fairy Godmother 69
Home again 71

5. READING ON 73
Learning to look 76
Learning to listen 78
Listening to baby talk 81

Appendix: Edward Salmon: 'Miss L. M. Alcott' 84
Works Cited 88
Index 94

I

Towards a Beginning

Over twenty-five years after the second wave of feminist thinking entered our cultural consciousness in the early 1970s, it is sometimes difficult to remember a time when 'his' was supposed to refer to both males and females. Or when we didn't think it odd, or even notice, that most educational, political, medical, financial and cultural institutions were ruled by men and staffed by women. Or when we ignored the fact that the texts studied in schools (with a few exceptions like Austen and the Brontës) were almost always written by white men, and that we could scarcely name a critic who wasn't also white and male.

I think back to my own history. I used to believe that I had 'done' a book when I could identify its theme, structure, point of view, and could cite appropriate authorities. When first studying *Great Expectations* in high school, I never questioned what the teacher said about it. In fact it never occurred to me to question either the teacher or her interpretation. So I couldn't help noticing the irony when, one day recently, a group of undergraduate students, struggling to turn their minds to textual analysis, asked me how I learned to 'think like that'. What they meant was how had I accomplished the shift from accepting an imposed version of a text to challenging it. Their question came, incidentally, in the midst of a critical discussion of one of John Burningham's picture books, *John Patrick Norman McHennessy: the boy who was always late*. We were discussing the full-colour imaginative life of the child set against the thin black-and-white angry life of his literal-minded teacher. The appropriateness of our discussion of the book to their question was striking.

The students' question, about learning to 'think like that', was useful: it made me consciously remember how my ways of looking and thinking had changed, and how feminist criticism had contributed to that change. I reconstructed a remembered story, and offered it as a kind of answer.

Penetrating the darkness

Walter Crane (1845-1915), renowned artist and fairy-tale illustrator, once explained, during a lecture to art students on symbolic representation, that the story of 'Sleeping Beauty' was about 'the hero penetrating the darkness and awakening his destined bride from her enchanted sleep' (*Bases of Design*, 238). He was reading the tale as a solar myth, and the prince as a sun god, awakening the world from its cold sleeping darkness. In Crane's own 1876 illustrations for *Sleeping Beauty*, he depicts the prince wearing a hat with flame symbol designs (like a lit gas ring) forming a sun circle around his head. What's the matter with Crane's version? In my pre-feminist days I wouldn't have questioned it and would probably have delicately suppressed my awareness of the sexual connotations. An obedient student, I would have accepted Crane's interpretation. I might have noticed that his comments chimed with Walt Disney's version of 'Snow White' (Sleeping Beauty's fairy-tale 'sister'). The coming of the prince was the climax of the story, and the story was defined by its theme song, 'Some Day My Prince will Come'.

In a more serious vein, I'd have recognized Crane's version of 'Sleeping Beauty' as an adventure-romance and would have taken my interpretations from Joseph Campbell's *Hero with a Thousand Faces* and Northrop Frye's *Anatomy of Criticism*. Their descriptions of a traditional heroic quest—as a dangerous descent into a thorny underworld, rewarded with a triumphant return, a princess and property—would have matched Crane's depiction of a hero 'penetrating the darkness'.

If asked to elaborate that interpretation, I would have suggested that the prince who finally wins Sleeping Beauty is a displacement or surrogate for the father/king who loses her to the evil spell of the spindle. I would have concentrated on the king/prince story and wouldn't have thought much about Sleeping Beauty herself. I wouldn't have been prompted to ask if the prince's story was Sleeping Beauty's story.

Now I know I read differently. I begin by asking a question: '*Whose story is this?*' Is 'Sleeping Beauty' about the prince? I think not. In the traditional versions of the tale the prince is a latecomer, arriving one hundred years after the main action. Nor is it about Sleeping Beauty's father. He is impotent; his attempt to demonstrate power by ordering the destruction of all the spinning wheels in the kingdom is a pathetic failure.

A second, equally important question: '*Who is the reader of the story?*' As a feminist reading 'Sleeping Beauty', I question Crane's interpretation. Seeing it as a man's story, a rescuer's story, Crane takes the male, active position of the prince, not the passive female, prone position of Sleeping Beauty. Which makes sense from his male point of view, but not from my female perspective.

To understand how these different readings are possible, I ask a question about the circumstances of production: '*When and where was the reading produced?*' Crane lived in a world which valued patient, passive women—waiting, 'immanent' women, as Simone de Beauvoir says in *The Second Sex*—as opposed to active transcendent men: heroic figures who bravely rescue helpless princesses. It is only recently that we've come to question passivity as a desirable female virtue. Think about the patient women historically presented as good role models: Griselda, who endures her husband's jealous rages even to the unjust loss of her children, or Kate, who is taught obedience in *The Taming of the Shrew*. Or think of the Little Mermaid, who willingly gives up her voice and tail for the man she loves, only to lose him to another woman. And he suffers no pangs of conscience or guilt because he had no idea what the mermaid suffered for him. The women are enveloped in suffering silence, which is to be interpreted as virtue.

In my pre-feminist days I wouldn't have given a thought to the passive unconscious form of Sleeping Beauty, or to the fairies busily vying for attention. I wouldn't have wondered what was going on between Sleeping Beauty and the fairies.

Now I concentrate on Sleeping Beauty, who is, after all, the star of the story. The father/king and husband/prince become the frame. I think about '*who acts*' and '*who is acted upon*'. And I re-vision 'Sleeping Beauty' as a story of a woman as a contested site, someone fought over by warring factions. In the end Sleeping Beauty wakes up, as Roberta Seelinger Trites says, 'not to a destiny that immerses her in her husband's life but to a destiny that is self-defined' (45).

The account of Crane's version of 'Sleeping Beauty' and my rethinking of it hints at how my approaches to texts and interpretations have been influenced by feminist thinking as well as by recent critical developments in cultural studies and post-colonial discourse. It explains (albeit obliquely) how I've learned to think differently, helped by questions about subject, reader and context.

What you see depends on who is looking, when, and from what ideological vantage point. Every text is open to a range of interpretations. For example, when I talk about *Peter Rabbit* with undergraduates, they almost always comment on morality and the justice of Peter's punishment, because in preparing to be teachers they are often preoccupied by such topics. But when I discuss the book with children, they almost always talk about Peter's heroic escape and how he gets away with being naughty—because that's what interests them.

Similarly, when I speak to a room full of female elementary-school teachers about Sendak's *In the Night Kitchen*, they quickly catch the visual clues that enable them to read the story as a birth myth. They see the Mickey oven and recognize the visual 'bun in the oven' pun. They spot other hints in the text about birth (the noises Mickey hears below in his parents' bedroom, for example). But they rarely refer to the point of interest among four-year-old boys: the aeroplane hanging over Mickey's bed and the heroic adventure played out in it. One group of readers focuses on one aspect, which another group elides, or slides past, in coming to a possible interpretation of a text.

It wasn't so long ago—sometime in the middle of the twen-tieth century—in an effort to 'raise' literary criticism to the status of a science, that texts were seen to have meanings intelligible to experts but probably not to the rest of us. Acknowledging and valuing multiple interpretations, or variable interpretations, is a critical attitude that has come to be very much a part of a late twentieth-century mind-set. This change in approach accords with a larger shift in cultural sensibilities. The shift is felt not just in literary criticism but in physics, chemistry, mathematics as well as in politics and economics: virtually all the arenas in which our lives are shaped. Broadly, there is a recognition of a shift from what are known as the 'totalizing discourses' of earlier in the twentieth century, to the 'complex relational dynamic' (the term comes from chaos theory) shaping our sensibilities nowadays.

There is nothing new or surprising about a cultural characteristic being visible only after its time is past. One critic attempting an overview of the shift from totalizing discourses to complex relational dynamics is N. Katherine Hayles. She explains that in science the mid twentieth-century push to find specific answers to specific questions faded out gradually, 'even in such traditionally statistical fields as meteorology and epidemiology' (xiii).

Meteorology is an especially interesting example. Does anyone remember when it was thought that accurate long-term weather forecasts were possible? Or that if drought could be predicted, it would be possible to seed clouds and produce rain? There were, in fact, attempts to make rain, but none succeeded. No matter how good the instruments, no matter how accurate the data, it turned out that infinitesimally small changes in temperature or air pressure (or any number of other variables) could produce quite large changes in weather conditions.

One of the most attractive features of contemporary scientific thought now comes into play. Instead of treating experiments that don't work as failures, scientists try to figure out explanations for what went wrong. So the push for fully accurate weather predictions, for example, was recognized not as a failure but as an impossible target, because it was in conflict with the fluid laws of nature. As Hayles points out, 'the important conclusion is that nature, too complex to fit into the

11

Procrustean bed of linear dynamics, can renew itself precisely because it is rich in disorder and surprise' (11). The perception that stability and order are unnatural changed the focus in several scientific fields, away from finding answers to questions towards the study of non-linear relationships.

In literary studies the same broad pattern emerges: a move towards totalizing discourses in the first part of the century, and away from them as the century ends. At the start there was a trend to tightening up literary studies, to give them the same kind of rigour and objectivity as the scientific method. In England I.A. Richards was advocating 'practical' criticism; in America John Crowe Ransom invented 'New Criticism', a term he used as a title for his seminal book on the subject published in 1941. Both critics emphasized rigorous, objective isolation as the key to analysing works of literature. Even the titles of such important critical books as *The Well Wrought Urn* (1947) by Cleanth Brooks and *The Verbal Icon* (1954) by W. K. Wimsatt drew attention to the classical elegance admired by New Critics. Absent from discussion were such matters as historical context, readers' responses, the impossibility of objectivity, and biographical information about the author.

The New Critical emphasis—on what goes on in the text to the exclusion of the outside world—was a product of its time. The totalizing effect of these discursive practices inspired a belief that scientific precision was possible, that questions of the universe were all answerable if just the smallest bits of information could be found. Theoretically, a text could be interpreted if it could be broken down into little bits. If each bit could be understood separately, then all the bits could be added together, one on top of the other, to construct a whole, perfect interpretation. Although this worked for erudite critics like John Crowe Ransom and I.A. Richards, it did so for almost no one else.

For much of the middle part of the twentieth century reading was taught according to the 'scientific' method of adding phonetic bits together. Groups of phonemes were taught, one after another, until, in theory, the new reader could string them together and become an independent reader. This resulted in large numbers of children who could read phonemes but not words. There were also children who failed to grasp the idea that words were intended to make sense.

Children taught in this way were faced with a different kind of totalizing discourse: the 'comprehension test'. These tests were made up of questions on fragments of a story. Correct answers required verbatim knowledge of the words—but often made nonsense of the whole. It was possible to answer all the questions correctly and still not have a clue what the story was about. In practice it also meant that students, in North American schools anyway, had to spend weeks, sometimes months, answering hundreds of banal questions, even if the text under consideration was short. To the dismay of teachers, despite months of 'novel study', students still didn't show much knowledge of the book being studied, and had little chance of acquiring knowledge of canonical (or other) works of literature.

The effects of mangled versions of New Critical practices still permeate schools. The students who questioned my approach to textual analysis had been brought up with New Critical principles—though they may never have heard the term. Students knew, for instance, that the use of 'I' was forbidden in formal essays, and that facts were desirable, while personal opinions were not. As an undergraduate, and later a graduate student in English departments, I understood the rules too. I knew that there was a body of material (a canon) I was supposed to study. To win an advanced degree meant that I had to know those books—from *Beowulf* to T. S. Eliot's *Four Quartets*, as Stephen Greenblatt and Giles Gunn suggest in *Redrawing the Boundaries*—and answer questions (objectively) about them on formal examinations. As recently as June 1984, during the oral examination for my Ph.D. in English literature, I was called to account by my (all-male) examining committee for the 'affectionate' style of my thesis.

At first I was puzzled by the question. I had just invested several years of my life in preparing a doctoral dissertation on the works of Ted Hughes. Why shouldn't I feel affectionate? And what did it have to do with my scholarship anyway?

Uncharitable thoughts about the committee members ran through my mind, but I answered in the approved academic way: by giving an authoritative account of the history of 'affection'. I began with Plato and Aristotle and moved on to W. K. Wimsatt and Monroe Beardsley's famous New Critical article, 'The Affective Fallacy', where they argue that speculation about an emotional response to a poem is not an appropriate critical reponse because it detracts from 'the poem itself, as an object of specifically critical judgement' (Lodge 345). They argue that the affective fallacy ends in 'impressionism and relativism', neither of which meet the rigorous, objective standards they set for the understanding of poetry. As I reached this point in the argument, I realized that the value of the reader's response, the affective response, was the very thing in which contemporary critics such as Wolfgang Iser, David Bleich and Norman Holland were interested.

The thirty-year move from Wimsatt and Beardsley's 1949 article to Wolfgang Iser's *The Act of Reading* (1978) marked a major shift in the history of literary criticism. Besides the move from New Criticism to a thicket of post-structuralist theories, there was a major change in what was being discussed. Whereas New Critics referred to 'works' (or poems or novels), post-structuralist critics refer to 'texts'. It is an important shift. New Critics began with the premise that it was possible to gain a total grasp of the meaning of a work. A text, on the other hand, with its etymological roots in the Latin 'texere', 'to weave', celebrates a process of becoming.

In writing about the texts of Ted Hughes for my doctorate, I wasn't willing to grasp his work totally. I even tried to end the thesis with an 'In(con)clusion', but the committee cut it out (though Peter Brooks, I notice, later ended one of his books with the word, without the brackets). I wanted to keep my affective responses weaving in and out of the texts. My affectionate response to the poetry of Ted Hughes was perfectly in accord with a sea change in critical response—though I'm not sure I articulated my position well at the time.

During the actual examination, I was lucky enough to have a

14

gift on my side: a letter from Ted Hughes himself in which he outlines his belief in writing affectionately, especially for children. In response to a question I had asked Hughes about his work for children and adults as part of a single continuum, he replied that 'one can communicate with children in a simple and whole way—not because they're innocent, but because they're not yet defensive. Providing one moves affectionately.'

Although I know intellectually that authors can't be trusted to tell the truth about their motives, I was delighted by Hughes's comments and deeply pleased to have the reference, as the committee conceded Hughes's 'authority' on the matter of affection. The academic committee's criticism of my affectionate style provided me with my own recognition scene. That was the last time I ever explained my affectionate style, or apologized for it. I realized that the presence or absence of affection had nothing to do with scholarship or critical ability and that feminist theory, which had fuelled my confidence in my textual pleasures, had other lessons for me to learn. Feminist scholars—among them, Hélène Cixous, Jane Gallop, Sandra Gilbert, Susan Gubar, Carolyn Heilbrun, Annette Kolodny, Jane Marcus, Toril Moi, Elaine Showalter, Janet Todd, Jane Tompkins—taught me not to exclude affection from scholarship.

Reading differently

Feminist theory is one of a cluster of discursive practices that reshape the ways we read not only works of literature but also our past, our present, and the way we imagine our futures.

Deconstructive theory, for example, helps us look at ways words don't always mean what they say. Reader-response theory teaches that what you see depends on how you look, and on who is looking, and under what conditions. Critical interest in the working of ideology teaches us to look for the cultural origins of assumptions about what is good and right or bad and wrong. Post-colonial theory makes us look at how beliefs in power and ownership shaped the societies we have inherited. Feminist theory—like post-colonial theory, like decon-

15

struction—offers alternatives to totalizing discourses. I'd like to think that these individual methodologies aren't struggling for something equivalent to 'alpha-male' superiority, though it must sound like that sometimes. In my own critical imagination I envision the current range of theoretical positions as analogous to those that shaped cultural changes at the beginning of the twentieth century, during that heady time, especially in Paris, when Imagists, Futurists, Dadaists, Vorticists and Surrealists (to name a few) were flourishing. No single manifesto became dominant. Though the individual groups disintegrated, something survived that we have come to term a modernist sensibility.

As a teacher and critic I am learning, slowly, to take notice of texts and ideas I couldn't see or didn't notice before; to question the approaches to analysis I used to accept as 'natural'. The questions I employ are changing too. The ones I now ask tend to be about relationships. Here are some questions I'll be considering throughout *Reading Otherways*:

— whose story is this?
— who is the reader?
— when and where was the reading produced?
— who is named? and who is not?
— who is on top?
— who gets punished? and who gets praised?
— who speaks? and who is silenced?
— who acts? and who is acted upon?
— who owns property? who is a dependant?
— who looks? and who is observed?
— who fights for honour? and who suffers?
— how are value systems determined?

The kinds of interpretation I look for have changed too. I'm not after once-and-for-all answers. I'm not interested in 'doing' books. The readings I find resonant are those that:

— offer a range of voices, some of which may be conflicting

16

or contradictory (Stallybrass, 4-5);
 — favour multiple rather than single readings;
 — locate the bias of the critic (instead of assuming objective neutrality).

Because I am interested in the ways feminist theory has changed the look of literary studies, I'm drawn to work that:

 — reclaims authors, especially those whose works have been neglected because they were out of sync with the fashions of the times. Christina Stead and Sylvia Townsend Warner come to mind. Their poetic prose fantasies are antithetical to the machismo of Ernest Hemingway or the epic of James Joyce;
 — offers re-readings or re-evaluations of works that had been deemed minor or of little importance (Mitzi Myers on Maria Edgeworth, for example).

While I recognize that feminist theory has significantly marked my reading, I know it is not the only way to read. And I wouldn't want it to be. What's important, I think, is an under-standing that critical interpretations are historically located and that they are malleable.

As a teacher, I want to be awake to a range of possible inter-pretations, so that when a student says something interesting, I can recognize a theoretical context. What I look for now, as I read, is a network of questions rather than resolutions to them. Relationships between questions are the current focus of my critical attention.

The problem with looking through feminist eyes . . .
is that you begin to see things you cheerfully ignored before. Not just in texts. Telltale evidence of feminist thinking (aware-ness of hierarchical ordering and the ways women are silenced, for instance) leaps out when you least expect it.

Several years ago, as I was walking down the hall to my office at the University of New Brunswick, I noticed a new mural painted on the wall, just outside the Micmac-Maliseet (local

17

First Nations tribes) Institute. The Institute was created partly to train Micmac-Maliseet teachers for the community and to foster traditional arts and culture.

The mural (slightly larger than life) stopped me. I saw a naked First Nations woman with a flower in her hair, kneeling at the feet of a man who was standing and dressed in a beaked headdress and a feathered cloak. What did it mean? Why was the woman naked? Why was she at the man's feet? Was she worshipping him? Was she begging for mercy? I thought about the way power relations work to keep women relegated to the bottom of the picture. But what if the positions had been reversed: a naked man looking up at a standing woman in fear or adoration? Or, instead of a man in headdress and cloak above a naked woman, what if there was, say, a white man wearing an academic cap and gown standing over a naked female student— with a flower in her hair? Though the general opinion around the building was that the mural was 'colourful', others in the faculty were asking unsettling questions.

As I looked at the mural a series of questions—influenced by feminist theory—played through my mind:

— *Who is looking at whom with what kind of expression?* I saw the naked woman looking with something between fear and adoration at the bird man. He appears to be ignoring her.

— *I looked at the hierarchical ordering of the figures: Who is on top?* I saw the man dominating the picture, vertically and horizontally. The woman is about one third of his size, and as she is kneeling, she is folded into a position of subordination—or worship.

— *I looked at the context of the mural: What is its relationship to its surroundings?* I realized that it was set close by an ethnographic display, of the kind found in museums. A glass display case next to the picture contains Micmac artifacts (beaded gloves, flints and the like). The implication was that, as an artifact of a long-gone culture, it was somehow acceptable to depict a naked woman dominated by a man. I found that discordant. It was painted by a local Micmac artist who is very much alive.

18

From a mural by Roger Simon
based on an illustration from 'The Chief and His Daughter'
retold by Eva Millier
Atogogoagann 2. Micmac-Maliseet Writers Workshop 1985

— I listened. What were other people saying? I heard a woman—I assume she was Micmac or Maliseet—talking to her son (about nine years old) as they walked by the mural. 'Do you know who painted that?' she asked him. 'Roger,' she said, 'Roger Simon.' I'm sure there was pride in her voice, the glow of pleasure that comes from sharing in someone else's accomplishment.

The feminist lessons? Simplistic protests about what's sexist and what's not won't do. I was moved by the pride I heard in the woman's voice and suspect this came partly from the fact that the mural was in a public high-status institution, a university. At the same time, I was aware that the artist had absorbed the ideology of the dominant culture as well as the ideology of his own culture. That's not necessarily cause for censure. But we should be asking questions about the relationships between cultures, and about the gender relations as played out in that picture.

When I first saw the mural, fresh from a summer of looking at nineteenth-century collections of illustrated fairy tales, I was reminded of Maxwell Armfield's picture of Andersen's half-naked Little Mermaid looking up at the prince, resplendent in big hat and long cloak. I am not suggesting that Roger Simon knew the Armfield picture. He didn't need to. Simon only knew what all of us know: it is natural for women to look up to men who stand above them.

There are plenty of examples that show how the illusion of man as superior in height is maintained: Michael J. Fox (five feet, four inches) spending hours standing on apple crates early in his movie career; tall leading ladies in old movies having to run in ditches dug along the beach so as not to appear taller than the men beside them.

Although it is easy to dismiss all this as silly, the ways people strive to conform to the tall man/shorter woman image, an inversion of the tall man/shorter woman order is still likely to attract attention. And I'd be willing to bet that lots of women at least think about not wearing high-heeled shoes if they are out with short men. Like it or not, the very fact of such large-scale

JUST IN FRONT OF HER STOOD THE HANDSOME YOUNG PRINCE

Drawn by Maxwell Armfield
for *Fairy Tales from Hans Andersen*
translated by Mrs E. Lucas
J.M. Dent, 1910

cultural sensitivity about who is on top means something. The 'socially peripheral' (relative height) is 'symbolically central', as Peter Stallybrass and Allon White say in *The Politics and Poetics of Transgression*. In the usual version of the 'normal' order, women look up to men: physically, intellectually, economically, and, in accordance with patriarchal religions, spiritually. Once I learned to look at the normal order with feminist eyes, I realized it wasn't necessarily normal or natural at all. It was patriarchal and hierarchical.

The problem with the wall mural is that few people actually saw it. The power play was invisible because it confirmed an accepted order: man on top, woman at the bottom. It was so normal that almost no one noticed.

RELATED READINGS *on* LITERARY CRITICISM
& THE HISTORY OF LITERARY CRITICISM

Terry Eagleton, *Literary Theory: An Introduction*. Oxford: Blackwell, 1983.

Gerald Graff, *Professing Literature: An Institutional History*. Chicago: University of Chicago Press, 1987.

Lawrence Grossberg, Cary Nelson & Paula Treichler, editors, *Cultural Studies*. New York: Routledge, 1992.

Peter Hunt, editor, *Criticism, Theory and Children's Literature*. Oxford: Blackwell, 1991.

Peter Hunt, editor, *The International Companion Encyclopedia of Children's Literature*. London: Routledge, 1996.

Christopher Ricks & Leonard Michaels, editors, *The State of the Language*. London: Faber, 1990.

2

What the Tales Tell

While reading through many dozens of nineteenth- and early twentieth-century versions of fairy tales in the Osborne Collection of Early Children's Books in Toronto, I noticed that though I was reading different tales, I kept seeing the same picture: a woman knee-high to a man. There she was over and over again, in a humbled or child-sized position: seated, kneeling, bent, folded, or, as in 'Sleeping Beauty', flat out, flat on her back.

On reflection, I realized I shouldn't have been surprised. Fairy tales are cultural barometers: stories without authors, always with us, always reshaping themselves with the times. The picture I was seeing was a sign of its time. But I still found myself asking questions. What time? When did that time begin? Has it ended? And does the picture of the woman knee-high to a man always mean the same thing every time it appears? I found I could approach some answers if I started thinking about my observations in the context of my historical knowledge about fairy tales.

The beginning of the nineteenth century marked the rise of the idea that fairy tales were suitable stories for children. Jacob and Wilhelm Grimm had published their *Kinder- und Hausmärchen* early in the century. It was also a time when European colonial authority over much of Africa, Asia and India was at its zenith. Maps of the world were coloured predominantly pink to illustrate British influence on large tracts of land. The order of colonial authority (white people ruling countries which were home to people of colour) was repeated in European domestic order (husbands in charge, wives and children positioned as subordinates). In *Guardians and Angels* David Grylls defines what that order looked like:

In nature, man ruled over animals, and God ruled over man; in society, kings and governors ruled over their subjects, husbands over wives, parents over children. To flout or confound this system of order was to violate God's decree. Part of Adam's sin was to put Eve above God. (24)

What I was observing in the Osborne Collection was an inscription of 'husbands over wives, parents over children' order. It was the natural order—and that was the one transmitted, at least partly because stories for children were supposed to be instructive. Without ever being explicit, fairy tales confirmed that order by repeating it.

The tales that are frequently reproduced in new editions tend to be the ones brought to popularity in the nineteenth century. They continue to circulate widely. When I ask students in a class to name the tales they know, their responses constitute the core of the fairy-tale canon: 'Snow White', 'Sleeping Beauty', 'Cinderella', and 'Hansel and Gretel' from the Grimm collections; 'Bluebeard' and 'Puss in Boots' from Perrault; 'The Little Mermaid' and 'The Steadfast Tin Soldier' from Andersen—and a very few others. A small group. Two hundred years later, illustrated tales are still the ones we usually give to children, and we still expect stories for children to be instructive.

As I broadened my reading beyond the historical material to include modern versions and films of traditional fairy tales, it became apparent that the stories and pictures changed with the times. I gradually sorted out some broad historical shifts, with critical insights provided by Marina Warner and Jack Zipes. I saw witches become less wicked, as authors and illustrators attended more closely to late twentieth-century questions of women and power: are old women perceived as wicked because they are powerful? Increasingly I found old women treated with more sympathy—and humanity. In Trina Schart Hyman's version of 'Rapunzel', for example, the witch is pictured almost as a wise old woman, rescuing a baby from a negligent teenaged mother. Instead of a wicked witch, an overprotective grandmother emerges.

I also saw a preference for passive women in the nineteenth century give way to a preference for the active in the late twentieth century. The emphasis on the virtue of the Little Mermaid's silent self-sacrifice, for example, fades as Disney re-creates her as a wilful American high-school junior actively disobeying her father: a California girl. The emphasis now is on her defiant spirit, something a nineteenth-century audience would have found discordant, but we find attractive. I know these are broad generalizations, but I am aiming for a wide-angle look at the changing fairy-tale landscape.

In this chapter I originally wanted to demonstrate some of the basic tenets of feminist theory by focusing on power relations as played out in illustrated fairy tales. It turned out not to be as simple as I'd planned. Contrary to my initial expectations I didn't find an inevitable progress from pictures of women at knee height in the early versions to active heroines in more recent books. Stories of powerful men did not simply give way to stories of 'empowered' women. History is messy. There are conflicting, contradictory influences shaping it at any one time. And these contradictions turned up in the tales.

Reading 'Bluebeard' stories was a chastening experience. As I looked through one hundred years of variants on Perrault's traditional tale, I expected to see nineteenth-century versions of moral lessons for disobedient wives change to late twentieth-century versions sympathetic to victimized women escaping abusive husbands. Wrong. Although the most common picture was, as anticipated, of Bluebeard's wife begging for mercy at her husband's knees, this wasn't confined to the nineteenth century. Here it is in a 1977 illustration by Martin Ware (page 26). Conversely, Walter Crane (whom I've just criticized for his patriarchal reading of 'Sleeping Beauty') portrays Bluebeard as knee-high to his wife. To my relief, as I puzzled over the pictures for a while, bringing my theoretical inclinations and my knowledge of the tales to my readings, I discovered that both pictures said a great deal more about the story than I had thought.

When I applied the question *'Who is on top?'* to Crane's illustration, I didn't get confirmation of the supremacy of the

Illustration by
Martin Ware
for *The Fairy Tales
of Charles Perrault*
translated by Angela Carter
Gollancz, 1977

nineteenth-century male. In the full-length picture Bluebeard's wife occupies about two-thirds of the page. She dominates the space as she runs up the staircase. Her upward movement confirms the justice of her flight, not the ignominy of her disobedience. Her backward glance at Bluebeard is one of pity (not panic, or even fear, I think). At the top of the picture is 'sister Anne', waving a scarf, signalling the rescue party of brothers, visible through the window above Bluebeard. Birds fly above their heads.

In reading the picture, I connect the billowing dresses of the pre-Raphaelite women with Anne's waving scarf and the flying birds. All are fluid expressions of flight and escape. Bluebeard at the bottom right, his sword raised, is echoed by the brothers in the window, whose swords are also raised. All the male figures in Crane's picture are partial, bottomless men. All have their swords drawn. Although Crane pre-dates Freud, those long, straight, raised swords signal male power. But Crane's placement of them in one narrow slice of the picture, off to one side, also suggests that they really don't have a chance against the big, billowing women.

Within the illustration:

"Come down!" cried Bluebeard, "time is up!" With many a sigh and moan, She prayed him for a minute more; he shouted still, "Come down!" "O sister Anne, look out, look out! and do you nothing see?" "At last I see our brothers two come riding hastily." "Now spare me, Bluebeard,—spare thy wife!" but as the words were said,

Illustration by
Walter Crane
for *Bluebeard*
Walter Crane's Toy Books
Routledge, 1873

And if I then go on to ask the question *'Who acts?'* in the picture, one answer could support the idea that Crane is showing Bluebeard's wife standing up for herself. She is not a model of nineteenth-century passive acceptance of punishment for disobedience. She is actively escaping, and enlisting the help of her siblings. She isn't helpless or static. Her disobedience is not central to the picture.

I'm not exactly stuck here, but I have reached a contradiction in my reading of Crane's work. How can I resolve his empathy with Bluebeard's wife in one illustration with his reading of 'Sleeping Beauty' from the position of a dominant male? My biographical knowledge of Crane helps here, and my preference for 'complex relational dynamics'. I don't need a final answer, just one that demonstrates two strands operating simultaneously.

Though Crane was working in a patriarchal, colonial world (and so would 'naturally' read 'Snow White' as a man's story), he was also active in the Arts and Crafts movement of the time, living a Bohemian lifestyle. He even illustrated a book for children, *The Child's Socialist Reader,* on the value of sharing wealth. What Crane sees in 'Bluebeard' is injustice, so it is not surprising that he sympathizes with a woman's flight from an abusive husband.

But what can I make of Martin Ware's 1977 begging-for-mercy illustration? It appears to be consistent with the early versions of a supplicant woman knee-high to a man. Yet Ware lives and works in a time when abusive men are subject to public censure. And Ware's other illustrations (I am thinking especially of his work in Christina Rossetti's *Goblin Market*) provoke a conscious consideration of otherwise suppressed gender wars. How could Ware produce something so apparently conventional? On closer inspection Ware's illustration doesn't conform to that conventional order after all. Ware is playing with a visual pun on 'see no evil'.

When I asked myself *'Who looks?'* (if I'd been dealing with a printed text, not a picture, I would have applied the question to the narrative perspective, to the narrative 'focalizer') I found no simple answer. Bluebeard looks out directly at the beholder but with distorted sight: one naked eye, one monocled. His wife is unseeing, shielding her face with her hand in a see-no-evil gesture (I've seen very young children use the same protective/denying gesture when, for the first time, they recognize themselves caught in an act of explicit disobedience). Bluebeard's hand, resting (where?) in what appears to be a casual manner, 'points a finger' at his wife: his accusing hand echoing her shielding/denying hand.

As Bluebeard isn't looking us 'straight in the eye' I find myself questioning the integrity of his position. Ware's illustration no longer seems to be depicting a colonial order that supports punishment for disobedient curiosity. He's pointing to something very unsavoury about Bluebeard.

Now I'm faced with another problem. Across a distance of almost one hundred years, both Crane and Ware recognize something suppressed in the 'Bluebeard' story. I discovered what that was by doing some background research into the history of 'Bluebeard' stories and by asking more questions feminist critics have taught me to use.

By asking *'Whose story is this?'*, I immediately stumbled on a

28

complicated answer. In the traditional tale a man forbids his new wife entry to one locked room of his house. She disobeys, and he uses his right to obedience as a reason for sentencing her to death. Though Perrault's story is called 'Bluebeard', it is not about him but about his wife. One nineteenth-century edition recognizes the doubleness by naming it *Blue Beard; or Female Curiosity*. The moral takes its cue from the subtitle: 'Bluebeard's wife had faithfully promised not to enter this closet and broke her promise: this was wicked' (15).

There's a second part to this answer: if the story is about Bluebeard's wife, why isn't she named? The reason was obvious, once I thought about both marriage and property laws in the nineteenth century: a wife was the property of her husband. A wife took her husband's name. A wife's unquestioning obedience to her husband would have been important in a society predicated on the colonial order of subjects obeying governors. Bluebeard's wife disobeyed and deserved to be punished. Crane, in his illustration, takes issue with the injustice of that situation, and so creates Bluebeard's wife as a person in her own right. Even that reading is not as straightforward as it may seem. In another illustration, as Marina Warner notes in *From the Beast to the Blonde*, Crane 'shows the heroine against a wall painting of the temptation in the Garden of Eden', thus suggesting that women as seductive and disobedient as Eve get what they deserve (244).

As I thought more about men's honour and women's rights to their own names and property, I gradually remembered something I'd forgotten about Martin Ware. His 'Bluebeard' illustration comes from an edition of Perrault's tales retold by Angela Carter. And Carter, as it happens, wrote her own contemporary version of the 'Bluebeard' story, a cult favourite, called 'The Bloody Chamber'. The property connection became clear.

The bloody chamber is not just a tomb containing the bloody body parts of Bluebeard's disobedient wives. The bloody chamber is a womb. (The literary term, incidentally, for this figure of speech is 'synecdoche': the part—in this case the body part—stands for the whole.) The womb is what Bluebeard is protecting, his wife's womb, that is, her chastity. In changing the title, Carter shifts the focus of the story: away from Bluebeard, or female curiosity or disobedience, to the bloody chamber of the womb and its significance as a place of honour.

I found I could go on now with my textual weaving—and unweaving. Carter's modern hint that 'Bluebeard' is about wombs led me to one of its traditional sources, the frame story of *Tales from the Thousand and One Nights*. The story begins when King Shahriyar discovers that his wife has been unfaithful to him. To make sure it never happens again he marries a new wife each night, and has her killed in the morning. On the night Shahrazad becomes a wife she saves herself by telling Shahriyar a story, stopping just before the climax. She does this every night for over three years. The fact that Bluebeard's wife (when she has a name) is sometimes called Fatima reveals a trace of the Eastern antecedents of her story, and the way in which honour and fidelity and protection of property rights are implicated.

As in the unravelling of any murder mystery, I'm now ready to reveal the solution. Although 'Bluebeard' looks like a story about the punishment of female curiosity and disobedience, there is good reason to believe, as the frame story of *Tales from the Thousand and One Nights* suggests, that the kind of disobedience in question is infidelity. Bluebeard's order that his wives not enter the forbidden room is a scrambled way of banning other men from that room, which, as Angela Carter names it, is a 'bloody chamber', a womb.

To a post-Freudian reader, Crane's drawn swords and the relative positioning of Bluebeard and his wife in his illustration suggest that he knew there was more to the story than punishment for trespassing. Crane's sense of social justice enabled him to bring into question Bluebeard's right to own his wife, to treat her as his property.

There is a little more unravelling. In the colonial period, during the nineteenth century, when many of the tales I was reading in the Osborne Collection were being circulated, and a canon of tales developed, ownership and property rights were important. 'Bluebeard' was popular because it upheld the right of a man to control his property (forbidding entry into a room) and to punish anyone who trespasses (his wife). Bluebeard's wife belongs to him, as do his home and all the goods and chattels in it.

Now the nested pattern becomes clear. Bluebeard's wife violates her husband's property. She trespasses into his private room. What that story contains is another story: Bluebeard's fear that the private 'room' of his wife's body will be trespassed by another man—a violation of honour, a breach of property. And male honour, as poet Adrienne Rich points out, has to do with blood, especially blood lines. If male honour is breached, blood lines are in doubt. And as property passes from father to son, there is cause to be concerned about the purity of blood lines, to ensure that they are not violated. Ware's depiction of Bluebeard's evil eye hints towards Bluebeard's dishonourable motives.

What I learned from my long exploration of 'Bluebeard' stories was that asking *'Who is on top?'* and *'Who looks?'* wasn't enough. I also had to look at the historical context of those questions, at the antecedents of the story, and the cultural conditions that produced them. I had to ask *'Who suffers for honour?'* and to consider how honour was determined (which led me to blood lines and property rights). Only then could I begin to understand the complexity of the pictures I was seeing.

Sometimes I wish I could come up with a definitive answer, a complete, foolproof explanation of what I'm reading (words and/or pictures). But literature is not like that. Crane's and Ware's pictures and Carter's story still fascinate me because I know they are all more complex than they look. The readings I find resonant 'offer a range of voices', even if some of those are 'conflicting or contradictory'—as are my readings of 'Bluebeard'.

Other ways of reading

My explorations of 'Bluebeard' variants taught me not to trust simplistic ideas of historical progression. My work with 'Hansel and Gretel' taught me something else: to notice who is reading—and with what theoretical lenses.

The most dramatic lesson I've had in reader-response criticism happened one day in an undergraduate class. We had just viewed Tom Davenport's live-action film version of 'Hansel and Gretel'. Davenport sets the film in the Appalachian mountains of the United States, hillbilly country, and uses almost no dialogue. The story is told by an American male narrator reading a traditional Grimm version of the tale. The moment the film finished, a woman emphatically announced to the class that she would never show that film or tell that story to her five-year-old son—because she didn't want him 'to be afraid of being abandoned'.

'But why? What worries you about the film?' I asked.

She responded at once, without hesitation: 'I'm afraid of being the abandoner.'

The bluntness of her answer came as a shock to all of us, and we felt its truth. Then this woman told us that she had come several hundred miles to take six weeks of advanced university courses, leaving her son at home with her husband.

Until then, I don't think any of us had ever looked at 'Hansel and Gretel' from the position of a parent, nor contemplated the fear of being the abandoner. From my own discussions with young children I knew that they focused on Hansel's and Gretel's cleverness at outsmarting the witch, getting the treasure and finding their way back home. The children I knew focused on winning. I'd never heard one express any fear of being abandoned. The closest I'd come to a child being afraid of the story was when one of my own sons informed me that Anthony Browne's version was a daytime story not a night-time one.

As I reflect on my student's story, I think about how important it is to take into account, consciously, the position from which I read. I know I read as an adult, but like the woman in my class I also read as a mother, and find (much to the annoyance of my critical self) that I sometimes want to censor what my young sons have access to. Fortunately my reading as a mother is mitigated by the other kinds of readings I bring to texts, many of which are based on who I am: female, academic,

Canadian, married—and other characteristics I probably don't recognize until a story I'm reading brings them to the surface. I also know that I can deliberately alter my reading of a story by changing my focus, changing my historical and theoretical lenses.

If I begin with the history of 'Hansel and Gretel', I understand that my student's reaction of fear resonates with pre-Grimm versions of the story. In *From the Beast to the Blonde*, Marina Warner notes that in the revisions to the 1812 editions of *Kinder- und Hausmärchen* the Grimm brothers 'substitute[d] another wife for the natural mother, who had figured as the villain in the versions they had been told' (211). Though the women who told the tale originally understood the psychological temptation for mothers to abandon their children (as my student understood it), the Grimm brothers in the 'romantic idealism' of their nineteenth-century telling had to suppress the 'bad mother' in order to 'allow Mother to flourish as a symbol of the eternal feminine, the motherland, and the family itself as the highest social desideratum' (212).

If I switch my critical lens, and bring, for example, my knowledge of Freud to 'Hansel and Gretel', I find my attention focusing not on the abandoning parent, but on the gingerbread house. In that most desirable of all fairy-tale houses I read the perfect sign for Freud's wish-fulfilment and anxiety dreams (228-9). The gingerbread house is temptation itself as it stands, an invitation, waiting to be eaten: the fulfilment of a wish, a dream come true. But it is also dream turned nightmare, an anxiety dream. The house is where the wicked witch waits to eat greedy children. There it is: the wish to eat and the fear of being eaten.

I'll admit to finding my Freudian reading of 'Hansel and Gretel' delicious. It is a nice, tidy reading that ought to leave me feeling quite satisfied. It doesn't. I'm still hungry, even though the house of temptation is a reasonably stable image in the tale, no matter who tells it, in what language, when, or with which pictures. Nevertheless, in the end, a Freudian reading of 'Hansel and Gretel' is as provisional as my student reading it as a story of an abandoning parent, or my children reading it as a story about defeating the witch. So I turn my attention again—this time away from food and towards money.

It was Anthony Browne who pushed me towards thinking financially. His illustrated version of 'Hansel and Gretel' calls to mind Marxist theories of the distribution of wealth, and the ways in which value systems are determined. Browne sets his story at the very edge of contemporary poverty, in a modern forest, removed from the comforting distance of long ago and far away.

When I ask myself *'How are value systems determined?'* in Browne's version of 'Hansel and Gretel', I see that his careful placement of consumer goods calls attention to Marxist theories of rates of exchange. Children are cheap and expendable. Goods are worth having. The Oil of Ulay on the dressing table and television in the (foodless) dining room are symbolically worth more than children—who don't need Oil of Ulay to look young, but who do need food. I find myself musing again on Peter Stallybrass's reminder that the 'socially peripheral' (Oil of Ulay) is 'symbolically central' (to the value of purchased youth-in-a-bottle over the lives of real young children).

At first, I didn't realize quite what the Ulay bottle meant. I knew it was something frequently mentioned by students in undergraduate classes, and it is the one brand name clearly visible. But why Oil of Ulay? Why not face cream from the Body Shop? Or Ponds? Or just an unnamed brand of face cream? It wasn't until I remembered that Oil of Ulay was advertised as a cream to keep older women looking young that I began to understand Browne's working out of the value system in the story: bottled youth is worth more than the real thing. I began to make connections with other pictures in the text, with the portraits of the witch and the stepmother as the same person, but the witch depicted as an old woman and the stepmother as relatively young. That raises the question of Gretel's kinship with the witch and the stepmother . . . .

But I've carried this reading far enough. And I'm shifting out

From *Hansel and Gretel* illustrated by Anthony Browne
(Julia MacRae Books, 1981)

of a Marxist reading of material conditions towards a feminist
reading that considers how women phase from maiden to
mother to crone. That's another story, but if you are interested
in pursuing it, you might want to look at the colour coding in
the clothes of all three women in Browne's version of 'Hansel
and Gretel'.

As you see, the story I tell depends very much on how I look.
None of these interpretations—abandoning parent, Freudian
wish-fulfilment and anxiety, Marxist material conditions, or

feminist phasing women—dominates the others. All are different from early nineteenth-century interpretations that sometimes served as warning examples on the dangers of greed. And I haven't included one of the most disturbing readings that haunt late twentieth-century readers: the spectre of Nazi crematoria hanging over the oven into which Gretel pushes the witch.

Now you see it . . .

I've been reading fairy tales for a long time now, looking at the pictures, and often discussing them with students in classes as well as with children. Some of the stories and pictures continue to resurface, no matter how many times I think I've finished with them. I know now that it was by trying, continually, to read these texts analytically that I was able to formulate questions I ultimately brought to my readings of other texts.

At the beginning of this chapter I describe my recognition scene of the recurring picture of a woman knee-high to a man. At first I thought I was seeing a representation of men dominating women. On reflection, I realized I couldn't support so static a reading. Martin Ware's Bluebeard picture, for example, made me recognize that the 'see-no-evil' and 'pointing the finger' elements in his drawing militate against a simple confirmation of Bluebeard's right to preside over his wife. I also learned to be cautious about linear ideas of progress.

Although I've concentrated here on 'Bluebeard' and 'Hansel and Gretel' there were other illustrated tales to which I kept returning. All these taught me to look differently.

'Snow White'. I kept coming back to Barbara Swan's illustrations for Anne Sexton's modern version of the story, Nancy Ekholm Burkert's 1972 traditional version retold by Randall Jarrell, and Fiona French's 1986 revisionist *Snow White in New York*. All three versions raise questions about whose story it is, and what the story is about. All three seem to be turning away from 'some day my prince will come' towards a story of young and old women. I ask some specific questions:

36

— Are there visual echoes in the placement of figures?
— Who looks at whom?
— What do those looks mean?
— Are the colours coded in any way?

Simple answers to the questions are never enough. What does it mean, for example, when Barbara Swan, Anne Sexton and Fiona French create Snow White and the stepmother as two sides of the same character? Readings in literary theory, especially feminist theory, help with answers.

Sandra Gilbert and Susan Gubar in *The Madwoman in the Attic* read the story of 'Snow White' as a beauty myth: the story of the ageing of a single woman, represented as a mother/daughter split. They suggest that the story pivots on beauty, its fundamental importance for young women, and how the loss of it turns old women into witches. Gilbert and Gubar see one woman caught in an unconscious quest for perfect beauty, the other in mortal fear of ageing: one woman trapped in a mirror, the other in a glass coffin. The apple which temporarily fells Snow White has one white cheek and one red cheek (a virgin side and a painted bloody side). Both women eat of the apple (with all its biblical resonance), but it is Snow White who falls, as Gilbert and Gubar say, to 'the female arts of cosmetology and cookery' (40). Gilbert and Gubar might have added that the Queen's two other attempts on Snow White's life are attributable to another pair of female arts/vices: the girdle and laces to couture, and the hair comb to coiffure. Once I recognize 'Snow White' as a beauty myth rather than a love story, I am able to focus my attention on Snow White and the stepmother rather than on the relations between Snow White and the Prince.

My readings of 'The Little Mermaid' make me think consciously about a bit of conventional knowledge that keeps surfacing in discussions on feminist revisions of fairy tales: the preference for 'active' heroines. I know that traditionally 'The Little Mermaid' is read as a story about selflessness, silence, self-sacrifice, patient endurance and suffering in the face of monumental injustice. But increasingly, as both Disney's version of her and this picture by Laszlo Gal show, she is portrayed as active. I ask myself why activity is better than passivity. Hélène Cixous's little poetic chart in 'Sorties' from *The Newly Born Woman* offers an answer.

Drawn by Laszlo Gal for Hans Christian Andersen's *The Little Mermaid*
retold by Margaret Crawford Maloney (Methuen, 1983)

Cixous argues that contemporary 'western' cultural organization is patterned on male/female couples. This is the pattern:

Where is she?
Activity/passivity
Sun/Moon
Culture/Nature
Day/Night

Father/Mother
Head/Heart
Intelligible/Palpable
Logos/Pathos.
Form, convex, step, advance, semen, progress.
Matter, concave, ground—where steps are taken, holding-
and dumping-ground

$$\frac{\text{Man}}{\text{Woman}}$$

The first terms are privileged: activity, sun, culture, day, father, head, intelligible, logos. All are masculine. Cixous argues that similar couplings inform 'symbolic systems in general—art, religion, family, language' (64). As I read Cixous at the end of the 1990s, I remember that she first published her poem in 1975, at a time when the 'binary oppositions' were in vogue. In the mid 1970s there was a fairy-tale fashion for 'active' heroines (of the masculine sort, understood as preferable). The preference for activity over passivity persists (*pace* Disney fairy-tale heroines). In feminist theory, however, a change in the interpretation of those terms is occurring, as my reading of *Little Women* demonstrates in the next chapter.

RELATED READINGS *on* FAIRY TALES

Ruth Bottigheimer, *Grimms' Bad Girls and Bold Boys: The Social and Moral Vision of the Tales*. New Haven: Yale University Press, 1987.

Marina Warner, *From the Beast to the Blonde: On Fairy Tales and Their Tellers*. London: Chatto & Windus, 1994.

Jack Zipes, *Don't Bet on the Prince: Contemporary Feminist Fairy Tales*. New York: Methuen, 1986.

Jack Zipes, *Fairy Tales and the Art of Subversion: The Classical Genre for Children and the Process of Civilisation*. New York: Wildman Press, 1983.

Jack Zipes, *Happily Ever After: Fairy Tales, Children and the Culture Industry*. London: Routledge, 1997.

Jack Zipes, *The Trials and Tribulations of Little Red Riding Hood: Versions of the Tale in Sociocultural Context*. South Hadley: Bergin & Garvey, 1983.

3

Reading *Little Women*

When *Little Women* celebrated its one-hundredth birthday in 1968, Elizabeth Janeway marked the occasion by writing in the *New York Times Book Review* (29 September), that Jo is 'the tomboy dream come true, the dream of growing up into full humanity with all its potentialities instead of into limited femininity' (Stern 98).

At the time Janeway's reading of Jo in *Little Women* must have seemed startling, even liberating, when compared with the usual tributes to the book as a model of domestic virtue. 'Women's liberation' was on the rise in the late 1960s and early 1970s. The term is long gone, now considered quaint, but memories linger of the revolutionary exhilaration it aroused.

Janeway sounds dated, her preference for the 'tomboy dream' discordant. Why should Jo have to give up 'limited femininity' in order to grow into 'full humanity'? Why should 'femininity' be 'limited'—or 'limiting'? Is it better to be a 'tomboy'? Does that mean it is better to be a man? It may have looked that way in 1968. If you are old enough, you will remember the dress-for-success look of blue suits (with skirts instead of trousers) that were considered necessary for a woman competing in a man's world in the 1970s. Those suits look dated now.

I want to be careful here, not to sound as if I'm shouting 'You've come a long way, baby'. Though I am trying to mark cultural shifts, I don't want to give the impression that today 'we' understand issues that 'they' didn't. Change isn't like that. 'Women's Liberation' caught the imagination of a generation of women much as the suffragette movement did at the turn of the twentieth century. The feminist wave of the early 1970s made a difference to the look of life in the 1990s. Government administrations, universities, medical and engineering schools, as well as law, business, and executive offices in Europe and America have lost their white boys in blue look—in favour of a more colourful palette.

In the last chapter I outlined how power relations play out (sometimes in unexpected ways) in fairy tales. In this chapter I consider how ways of seeing change with the times. *Little Women*, popular since it was first published, is a good example to use in chronicling historical shifts. By tracing characterizations of the book over the years I can see how criticism redefines what it is I think I'm reading.

Where to begin . . . with an obituary of Louisa May Alcott, written shortly after her death in 1888. An obituary is, after all, the first summing up of a career, the identification of a legacy.

Edward Salmon, a respected expert on children's literature at the time, wrote the obituary for *Atalanta*, a genteel magazine for girls. Salmon was actively involved in periodicals for young people. In fact, he had been corresponding with Alcott just months before her death, and she had promised to write a story for *Atalanta*, if she were well enough. Today, with Alcott in mind, I'm interested in what Salmon found worth saying about her. Did he wonder whether *Little Women* would be read a century after the death of its author, the ministering 'angel in the house'?

How does Salmon evaluate Alcott's worth? The entire obituary is reprinted on pages 84-7 so you can test your reading against mine. What I read is respect for Alcott as a writer, respect that is consistent with the ideological assumptions of the time. Salmon praises Alcott's work as a care-giver, for her nursing work during the Civil War; he assesses her writings as instruction manuals for girls learning to build 'small nests' in which to take care of boys. These are terms of praise, but they are also endorsements of the ideal of nineteenth-century womanhood. In saying that, I fear I may not be giving Salmon enough credit for his judgement of Alcott. After all, he also praises her as a reader (acknowledging her childhood intimacy with Emerson's library) and as a writer (even citing a story of her mother's

41

prediction that Louisa might become 'a second Shakespeare'). By examining what Salmon says we may glimpse how Alcott's book was read in her own time.

The Ministering Angel

In his survey of her life, Salmon dwells a little on her stint as a nurse during the Civil War. 'Miss Alcott', he writes, 'was one of a body of ministering angels who tended day and night at the bedside of the heroes who had fallen in the cruel crash of civil strife.' He goes on to say that her writing career benefited from it, and that without this experience '*Little Women*, and a dozen or more of her best short stories, would never have been given to the world in the form they were, and might never have secured their author a place among the first writers of her time.' I don't think Salmon was suggesting that Alcott's knowledge of war was of the sort likely to produce *War and Peace*, with its attention to the 'big' public issues of politics, war, and justice. Rather, as an extract Salmon cites from *Hospital Sketches* suggests, what Alcott learned was how to be a 'ministering angel', an 'angel in the house'.

This reference would have resonated with his readers in 1888 in ways we've lost. They would have understood the ministering angel as a close relation to the epitome of nineteenth-century womanhood, the 'angel in the house' who had been popularized in a very long poem (now forgotten in the popular imagination) by Coventry Patmore. The nineteenth-century angel is a good example of doublethink in action. Cherubic, a creature of perfect goodness, this angel is often portrayed as childlike or female, and constructed as a deeply caring figure. Even now, when we call a woman or a child an 'angel', we use the word as a term of affection or endearment or praise.

Biblical angels, however, were not soft. They were male, often warring (or at least fighting) active angels of death. They were macho creatures who, sword in hand, policed God's work. In the popular imagination of the nineteenth century, macho male angels were turned into wimps, locked indoors, confined to quarters and given the job of 'ministering'. Patmore's 'angel in the house' was like that: a double creature, an angel of life—and of death.

The nineteenth-century angel in the house tended to die young. In *Little Women* Beth is the perfect prototype; she is good, domestic, wifely, obedient and she dies after ministering to a sick baby.

The angel in the house exists for the pleasure of God and man. As Patmore says, 'Man must be pleased; but him to please is woman's pleasure' (52). His poem contains a catalogue of qualities desirable in women. I was reminded of lists of distinguishing characteristics used to identify birds. An angel-in-the-house entry might look like this:

characteristics: 'modesty, gracefulness, purity, delicacy, civility, compliancy, reticence, chastity, affability, politeness' (Gilbert & Gubar, 23)

natural habitat: the home

occupation: wife, mother, sister, daughter (paid work doesn't count)

Salmon's obituary follows this list of characteristics closely (with the necessary omission of wife and mother, as Alcott never married or had children of her own, though she ultimately raised three of her sisters' children). Salmon's focus is on domestic virtue. 'Miss Alcott's work,' he says, 'like Meg's "small nest," has been eloquent of home love.'

In Salmon's time the construction of the 'small nest' as 'eloquent of home love' would have taken a characteristic shape. It was organized in the pattern of a colonial society: a ruling, parental power and a subaltern, supportive body of cheap (or slave) labour providing goods and services. It was based on the interdependence of the couple: an active decision-making (male) partner and a domestic, supporting (female) partner. The 'small nest' of the family is still considered desirable today.

The March home in *Little Women* is a model 'small nest'.

Right at the beginning we are welcomed inside: 'It was a comfortable old room, though the carpet was faded and the furniture very plain, for a good picture or two hung on the walls, books filled the recesses, chrysanthemums and Christmas roses bloomed in the windows, and a pleasant atmosphere of home-peace pervaded it' (4). When the girls take a break from housework during the 'Experiments' chapter, the room instantly becomes 'lonely and untidy' and there is discomfort in the fact that 'Nothing was neat and pleasant'. Later, in 'On the Shelf', Meg's home is viewed as a desirable place, both by John's colleagues and her friend, the well-to-do Sallie Moffat, who says that Meg's house 'is always so quiet and pleasant'. The moral is stated at the end of the chapter when Meg learns 'that a woman's happiest kingdom is her home, her highest honor the art of ruling it—not as a queen, but a wise wife and mother' (399).

In *Little Women* Father (when he is not offstage at war) rules from the centre of the house. Marmee, from her corner, offers homilies outlining the proper role of 'little' women, including the repression of anger and delight in domestic work. There is no question that readers are expected to find pleasure and inspiration in the story. Every time I read the book, I'm surprised to find myself taking the housework homilies to heart: I attend more carefully to my husband, children and homemaking. I tidy up a lot. The tidy house is the desirable house, as even the little girls in Carolyn Steedman's *Tidy House* recognized. Salmon's readers would have understood—without having to think about it—the workings of a proper household order.

Salmon stresses that Alcott's legacy is educational. He reads her books as instruction manuals on the proper life. He dwells on Rose in Alcott's *Eight Cousins*, and glosses her line that 'girls are made to take care of boys'. Salmon assures us that Rose's message is Alcott's message: 'if Miss Alcott's stories serve to start young people in the world with an emphasized assurance of the truth of the view expounded by Rose, her books will have been written to a very high purpose indeed'.

Why is it that girls are supposed to look after boys? Or that female nurses tend wounded soldiers? Is this the natural order?

Atalanta and other nineteenth-century periodicals for children offer some clues. The first volume of *Atalanta* begins with a heraldic invocation by an eminent Victorian poet, Edwin Arnold:

Oh, girls! 'tis English as 'tis Greek!
  Life is that race! Train so the soul
That, clad with health and strength, it seek
  A swifter still, who touches goal
First; or—for lack of breath outdone—
Dies gladly, so such race was run!

Yet scorn not, if, before your feet,
  The golden fruit of Life shall roll,
Truth, duty, loving service sweet,
  To stoop to grasp them! So, the soul
Runs slower in the race, by these;
But wins them—and Hippomenes!

The story of Atalanta, the Greek racing goddess, is about the virtue of losing. She challenges prospective suitors to run against her; if she loses she is the prize. Atalanta counts on the fact that she has always successfully outrun everyone to ensure her single status. The scheme works until Hippomenes (with some supernatural help) throws golden apples in her path to distract her and slow her down. She loses the race. He wins her. According to the value system assigned by Edwin Arnold, Atalanta appreciates that being tricked into losing is really a way of being made happy.

Alcott alludes to Atalanta in *Little Women*. Jo and Laurie race each other. Laurie reaches the finishing line first, then turns to watch Jo. He reflects on 'his Atlanta, panting up, with flying hair, bright eyes, ruddy cheeks, and no signs of dissatisfaction in her face' (198). Jo doesn't seem to mind losing. The irony is that Louisa, in writing about her child self, says that 'No boy could be my friend until I had beaten him in a race' (*Alternative Alcott*, xiii).

I can't help wondering how much it must have cost Louisa to make Jo the loser in her race against Laurie. But by the time Louisa published *Little Women*, she had been earning her living as a writer long enough to know that she would lose readers if she disturbed the proper order. Like Atalanta, she knew that little women must come second—and show 'no signs of dissatis-faction'.

As I worked on Alcott and *Atalanta* and other periodicals of the period, I was aware that my view of them would have been incomprehensible to nineteenth-century eyes in the same way that the 'normal' of my world will look strange, perhaps even sad, to readers in the twenty-second century. But as I read nine-teenth-century magazines with late twentieth-century eyes I see boys (as represented there) looking forward to a happy life of noble purpose and adventure while girls learn to content them-selves with confinement and self-sacrifice.

Though at first I browsed widely, my attention gradually focused on bound volumes of *Atalanta* (it ran from 1887 to 1898) and on *The Captain* (1899-1924), a periodical for boys. I played about a bit, and found that if I linked the names together, as 'The Captain and Atalanta', I had the title of a romance novel—and a virtual guide to the proper order of gender rela-tions. *The Captain* is about coming first, *Atalanta* about coming second.

The Captain promotes winning, and devotes lots of space to gaining an edge in competition. Public-school life is under-stood as a training ground for establishment life in the public eye. There is no hint that private life should, even for a moment, interfere with public glory. Domestic and family relationships are unmentionable. In an interview with Henty, the prolific author of popular boys' adventure books, the only reference to his marital status is that he played cricket once in a married men's team.

Atalanta carries serialized domestic dramas, instructions on being popular (no whingeing about dressing for dinner), and some fashion tips (the art of hat-trimming). The absence of women's athletics from *Atalanta* seems a little odd, especially as the story of Atalanta centres on her running prowess. There are interesting articles on female artists and poets of the time, though contributors celebrate domestic skills and give short shrift to the professional accomplishments of the featured women. The emphasis is not on their work but on their roles as wives/mothers/daughters/sisters.

I found the same agenda repeated in other periodicals for young women. In *The Girl's Realm*, for example, there is a piece on Elizabeth Barrett Browning—part of an occasional series written by Alice Corkran on her brief encounters with the rich and famous. This story is one Corkran's mother told her:

> The poetess seemed to be all eyes and brown ringlets falling on either side of her face, a fragile creature that was a flaming soul. She took mamma into the next room, and, making a gesture enjoining silence, she led her to the side of a cradle where her baby slept, her "blue-eyed Florentine." Mamma never forgot the picture she made, as she stood there, shading the candle with her spirit hand, and looking questioningly at her guest. "Was ever a baby like unto this baby?" her eyes seemed to be saying. All her poetry, her erudition, seemed to drop from her before this sacred love, and mamma could only think of her as a mother. (277)

Mother first. Poet second.

Edward Salmon, in focusing on Alcott's domestic virtues as nurse, as teacher, as creator of small nests, was writing in this tradition. A century later, his terms of praise reveal, in the context of other periodicals of his age, a division of labour that looks like this:

Public Domain of Men	*Private Domain of Women*
power	service
coming first	coming second
paid work	unpaid work
job	family
self-respect	self-sacrifice

In Salmon's view, Alcott accords to this order. It pleases me now to believe she was subverting that order as much as she seemed to support it. She was, after all, a popular, highly paid author, working in the public domain.

What Salmon didn't appear to know was that Alcott was also the author of volumes of gothic blood-and-thunder adventure stories, of exactly the sort Jo writes and then recants in *Little Women*. There is a suggestion in Salmon's obituary that he knew something, but he represses the knowledge. Salmon writes: 'She found sensational stories pay best at this period [when she was poor and unknown], and wrote with remarkable facility'. But then he records that 'the then editor of *The Atlantic Monthly*, Mr. J. T. Fields', rejected a manuscript 'with a hint that she should stick to teaching'. In *Little Women* Jo uses the money earned from her writing to support her family, as Alcott did in real life. In *Little Women* Professor Bhaer encourages Jo to give up the unladylike, unworthy activity of writing sensational stories. Jo gives it up. Alcott didn't.

There is a delicious irony in the fact that Alcott had a palimpsestic (as critics Sandra Gilbert and Susan Gubar might say) career as a writer of subversive stories, the antithesis of the 'high purpose' Salmon claims for her. A palimpsestic surface is one that has been written or painted over twice, that is, a surface that has been composed upon, the matter erased, and then written over. The stories Jo recants are the ones Alcott publishes under a pseudonym, A. M. Barnard.

The fact that Alcott did write gothic romances is flaunted in *Little Women*. Then the stories are erased: Jo gives up her 'vice', and engages in the 'high purpose' vocation of writing moral stories.

When Jo meets Professor Bhaer she is working as a governess and writing racy adventures on the side for a local scandal sheet, so that she can supplement her very modest income. Professor Bhaer takes it upon himself to act *in loco parentis*, taking her father's place as 'household conscience'. The narrator of *Little Women* records Professor Bhaer's disapproval of the sensational stories printed in *The Weekly Volcano* (which had been fashioned into a paper hat the professor happened to be wearing during Jo's German lessons) and says that 'he only remembered that she was young and poor, a girl far away from mother's love and father's care; and he was moved to help her with an impulse as quick and natural as that which would prompt him to put out his hand to save a baby from a puddle' (354). Alcott was comparing her alter ego Jo to a 'baby' in danger of falling into 'a puddle'. Was that the value of women's work? Even by the time of *Little Women*, Alcott knew that her writing was paying the bills.

In the novel, when Jo's first story is published while she is still a teenager, she rejoices in the thought that she will some day be able to support her family. And when she does regularly start producing sensation stories, she equates the income earned with the purchase of material goods: 'one story pays the butcher's bill; another buys a new carpet; and another pays for groceries and gowns' (269). Jo earns money to support a family whose nominal 'head' is useless at earning a living. Jo carries on in her mother's tradition.

Louisa, like her mother before her, supported the family at a time when, as Salmon says, work was for men and nurturing for women. Louisa had to do both. Besides her parents, Louisa ultimately cared for her sisters' children, May's daughter and Anna's two sons (in her novel Louisa changed Anna into Meg and, anagrammatically, May into Amy). In order to afford such a large household Louisa turned her writer's hand to anything: from 'hospital sketches' (recording her time as a nurse in the Civil War) to gothic thrillers; from tracts on abolishing slavery and supporting the suffrage movement to 'moral pap for the young' as she describes her stories for children in 'Jo's Last Scrape'. She wrote over 270 works in all. That is a large oeuvre, not a small nest. In order to churn it out as quickly as possible Alcott taught herself to be ambidextrous, so she could switch hands when she got tired rather than stop. As Salmon notes, she often wrote for fourteen hours a day, every day for a month.

During the course of my research, as I read widely in Alcott's writing, I increasingly came to respect her intelligence. She managed simultaneously to conform to the social order and to subvert it. Her work was celebrated by critics like Salmon, who was looking for good, instructive material for children that confirmed the social order. At the same time Alcott flouted that tradition by being the 'man' in the family, by earning, by staying single, and by writing about conditions of women's work. Her stories of autonomous, working women spoke to people in her own time—and they still do.

Is *Little Women* still worth reading?

After exploring Edward Salmon's assurance that *Little Women* was a classic in its own time, I wondered how the book had fared among scholars and critics over the course of its more than 125 years in print. I turned to the Modern Language Association's *International Bibliography* of published journal articles and checked every year from the 1920s to the present day when I could access the information on CD-ROM instead of a volume-by-volume manual search. The results were revealing.

Scholarly articles on *Little Women* were few and far between. In the 1920s and early 1930s there were references to a few memoirs of Louisa May Alcott and to her position as a writer of a domestic drama for girls (three references between 1925 and 1937). There was a flurry of activity in 1938, the seventieth anniversary of *Little Women*, and perhaps the first piece of scholarship with reference to the 'psychology' of Louisa May, and 'a glimpse of the real Louisa'.

All through the first half of the twentieth century, however, it was evident that Louisa's pedantic father, Bronson, turned up in academic articles with a great deal more frequency, though his books even then were read mainly as historical curiosities. This fact clearly mirrors for me the household order of Orchard House, the Alcott family home in Concord, Massachusetts, now a tourist attraction.

On my first visit to Orchard House I noticed how small Louisa's upstairs room was, and how small her desk—especially in comparison with Bronson's large book-lined room and sizable desk on the main floor of the house. I thought about

Louisa, at five feet ten inches tall, writing for fourteen hours a day at that tiny desk in that low-ceilinged room. I couldn't help feeling that Louisa, throughout her life, must have positioned herself as 'student' to Bronson's 'teacher'. I was reminded of Louisa's description of Mr March receiving people who sought his counsel. He is shown as 'the quiet man sitting among his books as still the head of the family, the household conscience' (237). According to the tour guide at Orchard House, Bronson (the prototype of Mr March) used to waylay passers-by for hours of chat. People took detours in order to avoid him.

By the middle of the twentieth century, the articles on Bronson fade out. In 1943 the first glimpse of what might be considered the modern study of Louisa appears: the rediscovery by Leona Rostenberg of the gothic thrillers Alcott produced as A. M. Barnard. At the time no one was much interested. World War II had not yet ended, and New Criticism was in the ascent. A well-known American critic of the period, Edward Wagenknecht, writes from the perspective of his lofty critical position that *Little Women* 'may well be the most beloved American book'. In the very next sentence he states that 'it needs—and is susceptible of—little analysis'. In other words, *Little Women* is popular but not a classic.

It is not until 1968, when Elizabeth Janeway calls Jo 'the tomboy dream come true', that scholarship on Alcott picks up. Feminist critics of the period, through the 1970s and early 1980s, trained by New Critics like John Crowe Ransom and Robert Penn Warren, must have alarmed their critical fathers with their new taste in literature (a taste for rock music must have had much the same effect on their biological fathers). *Little Women* was hardly a classic 'well-wrought urn' in the tradition they understood, but I can see why it must have appealed to emerging feminist critics as a text ripe for reclamation: much read but little studied. Although it was known to be semi-auto-biographical, there had been little biographical research, little research on Alcott's papers or letters, in other words, little of the kind of scholarship in which academics engage when working out interpretive possibilities in texts. And with post-structuralist approaches, such as reader response and deconstruction, offering alternative ways of talking about texts, feminist critics found they had questions to ask about *Little Women* that New Critics couldn't.

Through the 1970s and 1980s feminist critics, including Nina Auerbach, Judith Fetterly, Elizabeth Keyser, Elaine Showalter, and Madeleine Stern, began to build up a body of writing about Alcott. There was a recovery of her work: editions of letters were published, biographies, and modern paperbacks of her writing, including two volumes of her sensational stories, *Behind a Mask* and *Plots and Counterplots* edited by Madeleine Stern, now available in a collected edition, *Louisa May Alcott Unmasked*. Other pieces of Alcott's prose have been collected by Elaine Showalter and published in *Alternative Alcott*. By the 1990s Alcott scholarship had turned into an industry. There were doctoral dissertations, scholarly books, new editions of long out-of-print work, and featured reviews of these reissued books in the popular press.

At first, feminist critics read *Little Women* either as Janeway's 'tomboy dream come true' or as the story of a victim, someone who couldn't make it as a writer, who was subservient to her father and gave in to the patriarchal order. Judith Fetterly, for example, claims that Jo never resolves the conflict between being a good girl and an independent writer, and suggests that Alcott suffered from the same problem. For Carolyn Heilbrun, though Alcott never managed to 'reinvent womanhood', she reinvented girlhood by constructing Jo as someone able 'to tell herself stories and to act in plays, in which she, a female, is the protagonist' (Stern 144).

By the late 1970s feminism was changing, looking for alternatives to patriarchal structures. Readings of *Little Women* were changing too. In *Communities of Women* Nina Auerbach calls it a book about 'a reigning feminist sisterhood whose exemplary unity will heal a fractured society' (37). In an inversion of the conventional order (where girls want to be boys), Auerbach points out that here Laurie wants to be one of the girls. He confesses his voyeurism: 'It's like looking at a picture', he says, 'to see the fire, and you all round the table with your mother, her face is right opposite, and it looks so sweet behind the flowers, I can't help watching it' (50). Later he wants to join the 'busy bee society' of March sisters playing pilgrims. He also wants to join their Dickensian writing games in the Pickwick Club. In a world that valued man-to-man talks and brotherhoods, Alcott created a sisterhood worth desiring and worth emulating—even for a man.

For Auerbach, to be a feminist isn't only to make it in a man's world (the tomboy dream come true), it is also to be part of—and to value—sisterhood. That marks a shift from the tone of the early 1970s when many women, especially intellectual women, stated a preference for the company of men, as if presence in a man's world was a mark of success. By the 1980s women were finding that a community of other women offered an intellectually satisfying environment, and they were choosing sisterhoods. In universities, for example, interdisciplinary departments of Women's Studies blossomed.

By the late 1980s, the view of Alcott as a victim was on the wane, and her life and work were now discussed with a view to discovering what they could teach. As I read 'The Ideal of the Educated Teacher: "Reclaiming a Conversation" with Louisa May Alcott' by Susan Laird, I felt I'd come back to the beginning of my critical tour of Alcott's work. Salmon had praised Alcott's pedagogical legacy: to teach girls to be 'the proper guardians of their brothers'. Susan Laird sees that Alcott was teaching something quite different.

Laird focuses on the fact that much of *Little Women* is about education, and some of it specifically about teaching. The teacher who strikes Amy is held as an example of bad teaching while Mr Brooke represents the good, though the kind of classical education he offers is without question available only to Laurie, the rich boy. The irony is that what Laurie desires is the kind of education the March girls create for themselves. Laird points out that it does not 'occur to Brooke that the playing out of classical narratives, home-authored play productions, weekly newspaper, and post office . . . could suggest educational strategies by means of which he might better engage playful Laurie's enthusiasm for learning' (281-2). Put that way, the kind of home schooling described in *Little Women* does look like the sort advocated by education experts in the 1990s. So I was delighted to read recently that Gloria Steinem too recognized the revolutionary educational practices available to girls reading *Little Women*. 'But where else in popular culture', she asks rhetorically, 'can young readers find an all-female group discussing work, art, and all the Great Questions?'

Steinem's comments were elicited as part of the promotional fanfare surrounding the release of a 1994 film version of *Little Women* starring Susan Sarandon and Winona Ryder. A range of famous feminists were interviewed by magazines and newspapers on both sides of the ocean about their responses to the book. All claimed to have read it as children. Some were embarrassed by their childhood devotion to the book, but Liz Forgan, managing director of BBC Radio, testifies that it could 'stay brighter in the memory than thousands of better books read since'. That *Little Women* can be characterized simultaneously as a story about self-sacrifice, domestic bliss, the autonomy of women, intellectual sisterhoods and problems of creativity in a patriarchal culture, is a mark of its lasting qualities.

Having read more of Alcott's oeuvre I understand more about the complexity of her mind than I did when I only knew *Little Women*. What I respect is her ability to have it both ways: to appear to be supporting the patriarchal order of her own time (and so earn money in an act of subversion of that order), and still to communicate her own desire for autonomy, her own creativity, across time and across space. In the late 1990s interest in Alcott's work is gaining further momentum. 'New' novels have been unearthed and published to popular as well as critical success. The list of articles, dissertations and books on Alcott continues to grow.

The current wealth of scholarship on Alcott and the new publication of her otherwise forgotten work have changed today's perceptions of her. The author of *Little Women* has taken her place as a 'foremother' of feminist literature.

RELATED READINGS *on* LOUISA MAY ALCOTT
& HER WORK

Janice M. Alberghene & Beverly Lyon Clark, editors, *Little Women and the Feminist Imagination*. New York: Garland, 1998.

Louisa May Alcott, *The Feminist Alcott: Stories of a Woman's Power*, edited and with an introduction by Madeleine Stern. Boston: Northeastern University Press, 1996.

Louisa May Alcott, *Louisa May Alcott Unmasked: Collected Thrillers*, edited and with an introduction by Madeleine Stern. Boston: Northeastern University Press, 1995.

Elizabeth Lennox Keyser, *Whispers in the Dark: The Fiction of Louisa May Alcott*. Knoxville: The University of Tennesee Press, 1993.

This bas-relief of Louisa May Alcott (1886) by Walton Ricketson accompanied Edward Salmon's obituary of her (page 84).

55

4

Carrie's War: Reading Feminist Changes

In telling my critical history of *Little Women*, I had more than a century of interpretations to play with, each taking about a quarter-century to evolve, changing as culture changed. Large shifts in critical readings of *Carrie's War* by Nina Bawden have occurred over a much shorter span. It was new when the second wave of feminist theory was new in the early 1970s. A cultural desire for definition of female heroics was emerging—something subtler than a simple inversion of the roles of prince and princess.

In 1993 *Carrie's War* won the Children's Literature Association Phoenix Award, an annual honour given to a book which sustains its critical appeal twenty years after its publication. That's one measure of its continuing success. In 1995 *One Week in March*, a survey of children's reading made by the School Curriculum and Assessment Authority in England, revealed that *Carrie's War* was one of the books read by *all* ability levels in the year 6 sample. The book sustains both scholarly and popular pleasure.

Besides my critical interest in *Carrie's War*, I wanted to write about it because it is a book to which I often return. Each re-reading affirms my faith in 'coming through'. The way 'through' is backwards, backwards through time. The secret pleasure in the text lies there: in the possibility of changing the past through reinterpretation.

Carrie's War begins with a dream of return— 'Carrie had often dreamed about coming back' (7)—and ends with Carrie's children running to meet her 'coming through the Druid's Grove' (142). The distance between 'coming back' and 'coming through' moves Carrie from uncovering a guilty secret to recovering a changed interpretation of her childhood. There is a resurrection of sorts, as people believed dead are found alive.

The frame story (of Carrie returning with her children to the Welsh mining village to which she had been evacuated as a child of eleven at the start of World War II) is set in the early 1970s, the time of its publication. Children reading it then may well have had parents who shared Carrie's experience of being sent from the cities to the countryside in 1939 to avoid the bombing. For children reading the book in the 1990s it would be their grandparents who had been evacuated during the war and their parents would have come of age in the 1970s, a period of increasing feminist consciousness.

The interior story, the one Carrie tells her children, is about her life as an evacuee when she and her young brother Nick were billeted with the ogreish Councillor Evans and his mousey sister Louisa, known as Auntie Lou. The outside story culminates in the expiation of a guilty secret Carrie has 'carried' with her for thirty years: that she was responsible for a fire that destroyed Druid's Bottom, the home of the late Mrs Gotobed (the estranged sister of Councillor Evans), and, she fears, probably killed its inhabitants: Hepzibah Green, a servant/nurse to Mrs Gotobed; the strange Mr Johnny Gotobed, 'a bit simpler than some'; and Albert Sandwich, another evacuee. My list of dramatis personae doesn't capture the magical hominess of Druid's Bottom, or the fact that it was a place of sanctuary, a place where people were well fed and cared for (by Hepzibah) during the hard years of the war.

At the beginning of *Carrie's War*, in the opening frame, Carrie struggles to explain to her children her sudden panic at being back:

Places change more than people, perhaps. You don't change, you know, growing older. I thought I *had* changed, that I'd feel differently now. After all, what happened wasn't my fault, *couldn't* have been, it just didn't make sense. That's what I've been telling myself all these years, but sense doesn't come into it, can't change how you *feel*. I did a dreadful thing, the worst

57

thing of my life, when I was twelve and a half years old, or I feel that I did, and nothing can change it . . . (13)

But the past can change, at least the understanding of it.

Outside the margins

In the genealogy of children's literature I think of *Carrie's War* as a transitional text. It marks a transition from the cosy adventures of children on their own (in the Nesbit tradition), to the complex family structures and social problems of contemporary Young Adult fiction (in the Jan Mark tradition). Nina Bawden wrote that she liked the idea (when I suggested it) and added that, besides being a transitional book, she had always thought the book a very personal one (15 June 1993). By 'personal', I think she meant not just the historical details (she too was an evacuee) but in the way this experience shaped her.

Though I know it is a mistake to read fiction as autobiography, it is equally a mistake to ignore an author's use of the personal in the fictional. Bawden's comments are, I believe, a way of correcting an earlier reading of *Carrie's War* of mine. In that version I'd tried to demonstrate that Carrie, sent to a Welsh mining village, was 'marginalized', using the term, in the sense current in feminist and post-colonial criticism, to mean someone excluded from centres of power. Bawden disagreed:

I have never felt marginalized by being female—only by being someone who always felt on the outside for other reasons. Having 'odd ideas', not thinking in a conventional way, and so on. I had a mother who took my education very seriously and taught my brothers to sew on buttons, not me! I went to Somerville, which is a single sex college where it seemed perfectly normal for women to run the world. Three of our old girls became Prime Ministers—among them, I fear, Margaret Thatcher!

Bawden drew my attention to the difference between being 'marginalized' and being an 'outsider'. The difference is subtle,

58

but I suspect Bawden was uncomfortable with the implication that being 'marginal' carries negative connotations: being an 'outsider' is positive.

Bawden says that she writes about outside children perhaps because they are 'inherently more interesting' as they are 'on their own, up against it [and], in some kind of crisis' ('The Outside Child' 694). One of her children's books is called *The Outside Child*.

In Bawden's *In My Own Time: Almost an Autobiography* she describes the various places she knew as an evacuee in her early adolescence (between 1939 and 1942) and how she learned to cope with the strangeness of being in other people's homes. By the time she reached her fifth billet, she says, she was 'accustomed to other people's funny habits' (43). Bawden speaks of the 'amazing liberations' that she felt in those billets, when she realized she was 'not being watched, *brooded over* by concerned adults' (54). Although she recognizes that her privations were negligible compared with those of children her age, especially Jewish children trapped in Europe, Bawden acknowledges that her forced status as an outsider served her well in the long run. She understands that in the narrow window of three critical adolescent years, she learned to be autonomous.

I appreciate Bawden's corrective on the difference between being marginalized and being an outsider. She helped me think again about the influence of feminist theory in my interpretations of her work. As I was doing my own research for this chapter, I came across two of Bawden's essays on *Carrie's War*: 'Through the Dark Wood', written in 1980 (when issues of gender and language were hot topics); and 'The Outside Child' in 1991 (when such issues had become naturalized). Nina Bawden talks about *Carrie's War* in both articles, often with the same phrases or biographical details. But what interests me is the shift in focus. The piece written in 1980 centres on a fairy-tale identity quest, while the 1991 article is about the complexity of human relationships and the exploration of family secrets.

The 1980 article haunts my memory because Bawden entwines the story of her schizophrenic son (who died after the article was written, but before it was published) with her story of Carrie. As *Carrie's War* is in part a fairy tale about going through the 'dark wood' and coming to the light, Bawden's account of her son seems all the more poignant.'

As I read the article, I found myself fixated on particular lines. Bawden says, for example, that 'fiction can be a bridge between the child and his future as well as a guide to his present' (68). She takes the dark wood (a common fairy-tale motif) as the physical location for a psychic journey: 'the dark wood is himself, the mysterious world of his unconscious mind and . . . like the brave knights of old, he has to get through it if he is to prove himself, to find his identity' (75). Except that she is talking about Carrie. The use of the male pronoun to refer to both males and females has become as unfamiliar today as the sight of a movie star smoking in a film. I understood that I was looking at an example of how quickly feminism has changed textual expectations. The pronouns are not the only things that have changed.

In the 1970s and 1980s the kind of journey Bawden describes would have been called an 'identity quest' (using the psychoanalytic language of children's literature criticism of the time). And although never stated, that identity quest was implicitly masculine—much like Walter Crane's view of the quest in 'Sleeping Beauty' as the story of 'the hero penetrating the darkness and awakening his destined bride'.

By the time Bawden published her 1991 essay on *Carrie's War*, the focus of her attention had shifted. Instead of emphasizing the archetypal quest she concentrated on the complex dynamics of human relationships. And instead of tracing the passage from child to adult, she writes of the overwhelming ideological forces shaping individual lives. She attends to what Carol Gilligan calls the different voice of women, a voice concerned not with the rule of law and property rights, but with care and concern for others. Though Gilligan's *In a Different Voice* wasn't published until 1982, nine years after *Carrie's War*, Carrie embodies that different voice. One of the functions of writers of imaginative literature is to articulate social changes before they are generally understood and accepted in the community. From the perspective of the late 1990s, I see that Bawden told the story of the 'different voice' of women some time before Gilligan defined the sound of that voice.

In my revised readings of *Carrie's War* I've applied some of the questions on feminist ways of looking about which I wrote at the beginning of *Reading Otherways*. They reveal a story about autonomy and independence, a way of looking that isn't dependent on a history of marginalized exclusion but on transcendent outsider-ness. As I worked on *Carrie's War* I realized that some, but not all, of my interpretations of the story were generated by my knowledge of feminist theory. Post-colonial and Marxist insights were in play too. I loved winding my way through these theoretical insights. And the cheering thing about this kind of intellectual exercise is that it is never complete: it is one more provisional encounter. The book will change every time I learn a new way of looking at it.

Reading *Carrie's War*

In answer to my first question *'Whose story is this?'* I turned first towards the title of the book, which itself offers clues to the book's ambiguous nature. Is it a girls' book? Or a boys' book? The spelling of 'Carrie' indicates a female protagonist, and carries within it an assonantal connection with 'caring' and 'care' giving. But 'Cary' is a boy's name too.

The title also announces itself a war story, and as war stories are supposed to be about battles between good and evil, tests of strength, machinery, and blood, they are usually designated as boy books. But as Bawden unwinds her story, she reveals battles of a different order. They are tissues of old wounds, complex prides and tattered rationales for puzzling behaviours played out by witches and ogres who are not what they seem. Fairy-tale quests are combined with ideological battles and gender wars.

If I ask *'Who fights for honour?'* and *'Who suffers?'* I see a story that works almost as a paradigm for Carol Gilligan's *In a Different Voice*. Gilligan's thesis is that men define justice as rule of law, while women define it by what causes the least pain or most benefit to all people. For women, justice doesn't have to do with property rights but with human compassion—with 'care, concern and connection' to use the terms preferred by the feminist educational philosopher Jane Roland Martin.

In *Carrie's War* Carrie struggles to do what she sees as emotionally right, not what is legally just. The political war, the theatres of war, the fights for 'honour' are on the outskirts of the story. Carrie always tries to do the 'honourable' thing, but that means trying to please others: Nick, Mr Evans, Auntie Lou, Mrs Gotobed, Hepzibah, and her mother. And in all her attempts to understand the ogreish nature of Mr Evans, she finds herself doing the 'wrong' thing. She suffers. For example, when she conveys Mrs Gotobed's message about 'owing more to strangers' (71) to Mr Evans, Carrie is horrified to find that he behaves as an ogre and acts, in his masculine way, to protect his property. Carrie had instinctively known that Mrs Gotobed meant that the other people living in her house, Hepzibah and Johnny, were to be cared for.

If I ask *'Who is named?'* and *'Who is not named?'* (the naming question is applied broadly and includes questions of forms of address), I begin to find answers that offer clues about the overt power structures in the book and reveal much of its intellectual complexity. Superficially, it looks as if men (Mr Evans, and later his grown son) are on top, and women, children, servants, and dependants (Auntie Lou, Hepzibah, Mr Johnny, Carrie and Nick) are at the bottom. Though Bawden subverts that simplistic structure, I'll read through it anyway.

Carrie and her younger brother Nick are children, referred to by their first names, as is Albert, another evacuee. So is the servant, Hepzibah. The 'innocent' and inarticulate Mr Johnny is addressed in a way that reflects his ambivalent position. He belongs to the Gotobed family and is addressed as 'Mr' in deference to his class. But as he is mentally backward, the 'Mr' is combined with his first name as if he were a child. Mr Evans is generally addressed that way or, even more formally, as 'Councillor Evans'. His younger sister, Louisa, asks the children to call her Auntie Lou (Bawden confirms that 'Auntie' was a common form of address used of adult female care-givers who are not re-lated by blood or marriage). Louisa's name is also literally diminished, to 'Lou'. The estranged older sister of Mr Evans, on the other hand, is usually referred to as Mrs Gotobed (that is, by title and surname) in deference to her age and rank as a rich, old woman. In the 1940s world of the novel, the hierarchical value systems are clear: men are on the top (Councillor Evans) while women (Auntie), children (Nick and Carrie) and servants (Hepzibah) are on the bottom. Mrs Gotobed occupies an ambivalent position. As money is equated with power, Mrs Gotobed was on top as long as she was young and well, but as age and illness erode her power, she loses control. Carrie's children, incidentally, children of the 1970s, are nameless. They are called, variously, 'the little ones' or 'the oldest boy'.

Although my discussion of names may seem unaccountably long and obvious, it underlines the power structure that determines one of the central plot elements: the threat of homelessness. While men have rights to property, women and children are dependent on the goodwill of those 'on top'. At the death of Mrs Gotobed, Hepzibah, Mr Johnny and Albert are threatened because Mr Evans wants to claim the property and turf them out. Servants are dependent on rich people. The children (Carrie, Nick, and Albert) can't do anything about the injustice, as they too are without their own homes, and without their own fathers.

Reading the power structures
So if I ask my question 'Who is on top?' the answer is Mr Evans. And if I ask 'How do I know that?' the answer is that he has property (the shop) and power. As a councillor, he is, as Auntie Lou says, a 'very important man' (23). As the brother of Mrs Gotobed, he inherits her property. The social order is marked. Mr Evans is an Old Testament prophet (his first names are Samuel and Isaac). But he is not a nice man.

At the end of chapter two, Nick says: 'He must be an Ogre, Carrie. A horrible, disgusting, real-life OGRE'. He isn't a fairy-tale Ogre, as the narrator explains at the start of chapter three, but rather 'a bully' (26-7). He demands silence, good house-keeping and obedience. He grumps if the women and children of the house sing, make noise, or walk up the stairs too fre-quently (lest they wear out the carpet). Councillor Evans lays down the law:

> 'Rules are made to be kept in this house, no shouting, or run-ning upstairs, and no Language.' Nick looked at him and he went on—quickly, as if he knew what was coming, 'No *Bad* Language, that is'. (29)

The brilliant thing about this book is that the patriarchal order is undercut. As Nick demonstrates, it is possible to ques-tion (in this case, with a look) that 'natural', patriarchal author-ity: Nick silences Councillor Evans.

Besides claiming the right to speak, Nick also manages to legitimize his right to steal from his oppressor. When Nick is caught with his hand in the biscuit tin, Mr Evans wants to pun-ish him—beat him with a belt—for stealing. Nick's timing is perfect. As Mr Evans approaches, Nick threatens to tell, to say he was eating biscuits because he was 'hungry' (31). The threat stops Mr Evans dead in his tracks. Later, while explaining the situation to Carrie, Nick observes that 'grown-ups don't mind being nasty to children but they don't like other grown-ups to *know* they've been nasty' (32). My son, at eight, made a similar observation one day when I told him that I'd just had a pleasant chat with one of his teachers, whom I'd found a very nice man. 'Teachers are nicer to parents,' he explained to me darkly.

The subtle undercutting of overt power structures pervades the novel and determines its ideological position: those who appear in authority, aren't. So in answer to my question *'What is the overt ideological position?'* I find that it is the authorized destabilization of the patriarchal order—a radical story for the early 1970s. This is manifested in the way Councillor Evans is cut down to size. Nick explains to Carrie why she needn't be afraid of Councillor Evans: 'you can't really be scared of some-one whose teeth might fall out' (28). The slip of false teeth from the mouth conveys the undermining of authority figures: an image of teeth without bite. Querulous and critical, Mr Evans roars like a fairy-tale giant, though he is just a windbag of empty Old Testament authority: Samuel and Isaac all puffed out.

The delicate complexity of Bawden's ideological constructions in the novel reveals her skill as a storyteller. I couldn't find simple answers to any of the questions I asked myself. Bawden manages to create Nick, for example, as a morally 'good' character, despite the fact that he talks back (the 'bad language' example), steals (biscuits) and ridicules (Mr Evans's loose false teeth).

When I ask *'Who gets punished?'*, I find myself in a 'world-upside-down'. That's a phrase popularized by Mikhail Bakhtin in his discussions on how the 'carnivalesque' works to transgress the established order. Nick doesn't get punished because he is able, as young children say, to 'use his words' (the classic tactic of the weak and powerless). Carrie, on the other hand, gets praised for being obedient (when she helps in the shop, for example), but suffers for it.

Just two pages after the biscuit theft, Nick says to his mother who is on a visit, that 'Mr. Evans cheats when he counts saccharine tablets' (37). Carrie was actually relieved that this is all Nick had said. In the preceding moments Carrie—in her concern, her care, for others—was afraid

> that any minute now he [Nick] would come out with it, that he'd say he hated Mr Evans and not being allowed to use the bathroom in the daytime, even when it was cold. That he hated the cold and his chilblains and the earth privy and the spiders and not being allowed to eat biscuits and only having roast beef for dinner because *she* had come. Carrie would have died rather than say these things but Nick wouldn't be embarrassed. . . .What she [Carrie] did mind—minded quite horribly—was that it would upset Auntie Lou. (37)

Carrie's silence is motivated by not wanting to hurt anyone's feelings, her recognition of her low-order position. Here

Bawden has created the moral dilemma: Carrie does the 'right' thing and suffers, while Nick does the 'wrong' thing and benefits. The resolution isn't what matters; rather it is the way in which Bawden makes the reader aware of the characters' ambiguous behaviour and its causes.

My questions 'Who speaks?' and 'Who is silenced?' reveal the dialectical dance within the novel. Nick wins because he uses the system to his advantage. Carrie, concerned with the feelings of others, is often silenced. But towards the end of the book, when Albert realizes that he can't prevent the evictions of Hepzibah and Mr Johnny, he articulates the relationships between speech and action in a world where children are conventionally seen but not heard: 'It's a fearful *handicap* being a child. You have to stand there and watch, you can never make anything happen. Or stop things you don't like. If I was a grown-up, I could stop *this*' (116). What is startling about Albert's observation is that it puts a twist on the answer to 'Who looks?' and 'Who is observed?' Bawden recognizes that children watch, and observe adult injustice. Bawden also acknowledges their deep shame at being able to look but not act.

Albert's complaint that as a child he has 'to stand there and watch' opens another fundamental aspect of the way power structures are played out in the book. As a child, Albert feels invisible. Carrie feels the same helplessness. The idea that children are the watchers destabilizes a feminist generalization that women and children are regarded as 'objects', primarily 'objects of desire'. Yet in *Carrie's War* the ability of children to watch and see what is going on becomes an asset. Nick knows that something special is going on with Aunt Lou. He can read the situation, and knows how to keep it a secret.

Once the power structure is made visible, other questions come into focus: 'Who acts?' and 'Who is acted upon?' Now the heart of Carrie's 'war' is revealed. The one act that she regrets, the one she wishes she could change, the 'dreadful thing', the 'worst thing' in her life, was committed when she was twelve and a half years old. What she did was throw a skull out of a window. That was the act—but its significance is only clear within a certain context. What is wrong with throwing a skull out a window? But what is a skull doing near a window in the first place? And why is that such a bad thing? In the answers lie a history of colonial exploitation, a helplessness of exploited slaves paralleled by exploited children, women and old people exploited by men. The story behind the skull being thrown out of the window has three phases, one layered on the other. In the oldest layer is the skull itself.

The skull is the focus of one of Hepzibah's stories. In her telling of the legend the skull belonged to a young African boy, a slave, who was brought to Druid's Bottom when the family was making its money in 'sugar and slaves' (52), during the colonial exploitation of Africa. Even though, Hepzibah assures us, the child was well taken care of, he cried and wanted to go home. The family promised he could, but he died the first winter, making them feel they'd broken their promise. According to Hepzibah, 'he put a curse on the house', asking that, after he had been buried, they would 'dig up his skull and keep it in the house or some dreadful disaster would come. The walls would crumble' (53). And when someone had tried to dispose of the skull, there was a visitation and every mirror in the house cracked. The African child of the story had been 'acted upon' by being forcibly removed to be an ornament of the Gotobed family. His act (putting the curse on the house) was a way of evening up the score after his displacement from his homeland. No one had attempted to dispose of the skull again—until Carrie did.

The second level of action moves closer to Carrie's story and explains Mr Evans's actions: Mr Evans is mean because he was meanly treated. He wants to dispossess others because he feels dispossessed. He acts as he does (in his desire to claim the property), says Hepzibah, because 'He's had a cold, hard life and it's made him cold and hard' (81). Mr Evans saw his father killed in the mine owned by the Gotobeds (who were bad owners) and vowed never to go back. So he worked to buy his own shop, raise his son and much younger sister, and look after his sickly wife. He resented his older sister, Dilys (Mrs Gotobed), because she consorted with the enemy, marrying into the family of mine-owners who were responsible for the death of her father: 'she rose up in the world without lifting a finger when she married into the gentry' (81).

Though Nina Bawden creates Mr Evans as a capitalist monster, he is complicated by left-wing leanings. He has worked for his own middle-class existence, and so is untainted by the ease of the inherited wealth of the mine-owners, people who bought their leisure at the expense of the labour of others. As Bawden herself says, she was bothered by the way the adults in the books of her childhood were 'emotionally hygienic'. Yet when Carrie throws the skull out of the window, she is casting her lot with the cycle of dispossession: she is trying to invoke the curse, to dispossess Mr Evans, the way he intends to dispossess Johnny and Hepzibah.

Hepzibah's explanation of the history of Mr Evans changes Carrie's interpretation of the present, and shifts the focus away from Mr Evans as totally bad towards sympathy for him. Sympathy for old, sick, impoverished Mrs Gotobed drains away in proportion. A Marxist shadow hangs over the whole. The rich exploit the poor and the poor retaliate. Property and ownership are at the heart of the story.

Mr Evans inherits Druid's Bottom and wants to dispossess Hepzibah and Mr Johnny. They are acted upon, and Mr Evans acts. Which brings me to the third layer—Carrie throws the skull out the window in frustrated rage at being powerless in a distressing situation. She cannot stop Mr Evans from dispossessing Hepzibah and Mr Johnny, and she feels, guiltily, that she is in some way the cause of the dispossession, that she has misrepresented the last wishes of Mrs Gotobed. She acts because she can't change the ways in which she has been deprived, of parents, of home, of the comfort and warmth of Hepzibah's kitchen.

Each layer of the story is linked to issues of death and property. The African boy dies offering the curse as a talisman against future dispossession. Mrs Gotobed dies and tries (at least we are to believe she tries) to ensure that Hepzibah and Mr Johnny are not dispossessed. Carrie, helpless to stop this, throws the skull out the window, and believes she has caused three deaths. At the end of the novel, though Carrie's recognition scene occurs off-stage, the presumed-dead Hepzibah and Mr Johnny return, along with the news that Albert is alive too.

There is one more layer to the cycle of death, an oblique ripple that surrounds the story but is outside it. Carrie's husband, an archaeologist (appropriately), has died, so Carrie and her children are, by chance, visiting the scene of her own loss and dispossession. Though she can't resurrect her husband and the father of her children, she does resurrect that other family from the past. Carrie experiences the same kind of rage felt by Mr Evans when he saw his father killed and couldn't help, and by the African boy who was taken from his home and couldn't get back. Both were acted upon, both dispossessed, both victims of economic and social forces over which they had no control.

Carrie's act of defiance is an attempt to spite the history of dispossession. And so I'm answering more questions: *'Who owns property?'* and *'Who doesn't own property?'* Owners eventually lose their property to the masses. The crimes of long-dead slave-owners and mine-owners are expiated. In the end, Hepzibah and Mr Johnny inherit by default. The dead house rises from the ashes.

The property question leads to another: *'How are value systems determined?'* I'm again conscious of the complexity of the novel, as two entwined value systems are played out; one takes its cues from fairy tales; the other from Marxist views of property.

The Witch and the Fairy Godmother

On the first page of *Carrie's War*, Bawden hints that this will be a new kind of fairy tale as she plunges Carrie into what seems to be a fairy-tale forest, through yew trees (traditionally death trees), 'dark green and so old that they had grown twisted and lumpy, like arthritic fingers' (7). That is the phantom forest haunting Carrie's nightmares: 'the fingers reached out for her, plucking at her hair and her skirt as she ran' (7). The daytime forest Carrie finds when she enters it with her children is quite different. It is fragrant, welcoming, a flourishing wild garden of 'blackberries and wild rose and hazelnut bushes' (7). There are no 'grabbing' trees; instead, Carrie and her children are in control—like the fairy-tale prince who enjoys divine protection. The narrator makes the connection clear: 'it was like pushing through a forgotten forest in a fairy tale. The tangled wood round Sleeping Beauty's castle' (7). This gentle passage makes explicit the kind of changed sensibility that feminist writers sought but rarely achieved in the 1970s. Their heavy-handed princess-rescues-prince inversions rarely celebrated the joys of feminine autonomy.

Bawden's placement of Carrie and her children as the 'prince' figure is very much in the spirit of Carolyn Heilbrun's Snow White thesis: that the prince is really Snow White waking herself up, her own animus, her masculine self in disguise. Even here, the subtle expression of *Carrie's War* as a resurrection story is carried through. 'Sleeping Beauty' is, after all, a story about death and rebirth, as reiterated in Bawden's choice of flora: deadly yew trees are transformed into nourishing fruit (blackberries and hazelnuts) and beautiful flowers.

In the feminist fairy-tale interpretation, if Carrie is a revisionist female protagonist who wakes herself up, then Hepzibah is a revised witch. In nineteenth-century fairy tales, as retold by the Grimm brothers, old women, especially stepmothers, are often powerful, dangerous and evil. Think of 'Hansel and Gretel'. Hepzibah is the witch in *Carrie's War*, but she is the reclaimed feminist witch, the good witch, the healer, the henwife. Hepzibah keeps the kitchen bright and warm, cooks wonderful food, tells stories, hugs children and heals chilblains. Though the house appears to be at the heart of a dangerous forest, cut off and in decline, it is a place of rebirth. There is even a scene describing the birth of a cow, included as Nick's 'best thing'. And at the end, Hepzibah and Mr Johnny rise from the interior story into the frame story, as they rise from behind the ashes and ruin of the old house.

Let me just run through the ways in which Bawden reinvents

the traditional iconography of the fairy tale. Hepzibah would have been the witch in a nineteenth-century telling of the fairy tale; Bawden makes her the fairy godmother. Carrie, who would have been the Gretel figure, finds herself resurrecting, not destroying, the witch. Indirectly, she allows Hepzibah and Mr Johnny to live happily ever after. What Carrie has assumed to be an act of destruction, in fact restores the house to its rightful inheritors. In the end, the weak inherit, the outsider copes, the 'different' voice of feminine 'caring' restores social order.

Home again

The emphasis on home and property rights points to the heart of distinctions between feminist and patriarchal cultures. Feminist texts are about private space, home, and nurturing, while male-order books are about public space, ownership and winning. In *Carrie's War* the reader encounters the two agendas presented in a way that identifies the book as 'transitional', one on the cusp of the feminist changes which have transformed European and American culture since the early 1970s.

Every time I reread *Carrie's War*, I am impressed anew by the complexity of the intertextual relations within it. With every new question I bring to the text, I open a different vein of interpretive possibilities. My questions about property led me to Marxist ideas of material culture. In discussing the book I can focus on people being dispossessed: Hepzibah, Mr Johnny, Carrie, Nick, and the legend of the skull of the African boy. Or I can talk about property in relation to the Gotobed family as slave- owners, then as bad mine-owners, and to Mr Evans as a greedy, patriarchal ogre.

Or I can concentrate on feminist questions of hierarchical ordering, of a 'different voice', of the difference between being marginalized and being an outsider. That leads me to discussions of Carrie's attempts to fathom the mysteries of human nature— while not hurting anyone's feelings. And feminist questions of speech and silence, of names and namelessness, of honour and suffering, show how Mr Evans exploits his younger sister Louisa and tries to keep her silenced and indoors.

71

And if I return to *Carrie's War* as a revisionist fairy tale I see it as a story of death and resurrection. I see Mr Johnny, Hepzibah and Albert Sandwich being reborn out of the deaths that haunt the story: the death of Carrie's husband, of the African children, and the offstage deaths of World War II. All the stories weave together in a complex relational dynamic of interpretive possibilities. And I know there are other readings out there, waiting for someone else to find.

RELATED READINGS *on* COMING OF AGE

Rachel Brownstein, *Becoming a Heroine: Reading about Women in Novels* (1982). Harmondsworth: Penguin, 1984.

Jill Ker Conway, *The Road from Coorain* (1989). New York: Vintage, 1990.

Margaret Mahy, *The Changeover: A Supernatural Romance*. London: Dent, 1984.

Tim Wynne-Jones, *The Maestro*. Toronto: Douglas & McIntyre, 1995.

5

Reading On

As I was coming to the end of writing this book, I happened to be reading *Alice Through the Looking-Glass* to my sons. At the beginning of the second chapter, I was surprised by a sudden surge of empathy with Alice as she tries to attain a wide-angle view of a tantalizing, desirable garden:

'I should see the garden far better,' said Alice to herself, 'if I could get to the top of that hill: and here's a path that leads straight to it—at least, no, it doesn't do *that* . . .'

Every time Alice tries to take the straight path to the top, you remember, she finds she can't get anywhere. Only by resolutely 'walking in the opposite direction' does she achieve the longed-for hill and find herself able to appreciate the view.

I know the *Alice* books intimately, but for the first time was shaken by my feeling of connection with Alice's failed attempts to take the straight route to the top. Even though I had understood, from the time I began *Reading Otherways*, that it was futile to attempt to validate a set of hard-wired feminist characteristics, or to try to prove the primacy of feminist theory in the literary-criticism sweepstakes, I still didn't expect all my readings to be quite so circuitous. In fact, it was only towards the end of the writing, when asked to summarize *Reading Otherways*, that I found myself answering that it was about getting readings wrong and working out correctives. That was only partly a joke. Feminist criticism was changing the category of children's literature even as I was writing. And I was discovering—as Alice does in her encounter with the pig/baby—how hard it is to get a grip on shape-shifters.

The problem with texts, as critic Mary Louise Pratt says in *Imperial Eyes*, is that 'to be read [they have] to be readable' (4). Although she is talking about the difficulty of reading a 1200-page manuscript from the early seventeenth century, written in a mixture of Quechua (a South American dialect) and rough Spanish, which turned up at the beginning of the twentieth century in a library in Copenhagen, she is also talking about cultural readability. Her point is that colonizing Europeans couldn't, until very recently, hear the voices of the people they colonized—let alone their versions of colonial encounters. The manuscript only became translatable, its cultural significance visible, late in the twentieth century.

Problems of readability and cross-cultural encounters aren't restricted to historical curiosities in foreign languages. Examples of what Pratt calls transculturation—'how subordinated or marginal groups select and invent from materials transmitted to them by a dominant or metropolitan culture' (6)—occur today and close to home. In fact, a perfect example of transculturation took place in one of my graduate classes at the University of New Brunswick. An apparently simple text enabled us to cross borders of language, age, culture, gender, home and school—and learn to hear a song we'd not quite forgotten but nevertheless had firmly consigned to the lower regions of the repertoire. In order to read that text, we had to learn to think differently about it, to ask questions we'd not thought to ask before.

A kindergarten teacher, Peter Gorham, brought in *"More More More," Said the Baby: 3 Love Stories*, a picture book for very young children written and illustrated by Vera B. Williams. Each nursery-verse vignette offers a glimpse of an adult playing with a toddler: first 'daddy' and 'Little Guy' (both white); then (white) 'grandma' and (black) 'Little Pumpkin'; and finally (Asian) 'mama' and 'Little Bird'. The multicultural agenda was clear enough to all of us. It felt right, in tune with contemporary cultural sensibilities. But the students felt that something disturbing, something not quite readable, was there too. So we began to read, exploring the story, to see if we could locate the source of unease. We began with daddy talking to Little Guy:

74

"Just look at you
with your perfect belly button

right in the middle
right in the middle
right in the middle
of your fat little belly".

Then Little Guy's daddy
brings that baby
right up close

and gives that little guy's belly
a kiss right in the middle
of the belly button.

Peter recognized, at least initially, something not quite suited
to school when he read *"More More More"* to the four- and five-
year-olds in his class. He knew there was something slightly
transgressive, perhaps voyeuristic in revealing intimate domestic
moments in a classroom. The first story of kissing the baby's
belly seemed risqué enough. The second even more so. In that
one the grandmother 'tastes' each of Little Pumpkin's 'ten little
toes'. The third story returns to a safer zone as the mother kisses
the closed eyes of the sleeping Little Bird.

Peter knew intuitively that he brought *"More More More"* to
our graduate class because it served as a kind of gloss, almost an
explanation of the theoretical text I had assigned that day: *Bitter
Milk* by Madeline Grumet, a philosophical book on curriculum
theory, dealing with the way teachers, especially teachers of
young children, negotiate between authoritative (disciplined)
schooled discourses and nurturing (playful) maternal peda-
gogies. But the connection between theory and text remained
elusive, even though Peter is an active member of a Maternal
Literacies Group (made up of parents, teachers and academics),
which studies home/school relations. All the clues needed to

75

make sense of the text were there, of course, waiting to be found. We continued to examine the evidence, and attempted to record our observations of what we were seeing.

Learning to look

The images, the scenes, in *"More More More"* are routine to anyone who plays with infants. It is almost as if the reader is spying through a window on a private but familiar event. The sensual, verging on sexual imagery of kissing belly buttons, toes and eyes is a nurturing form of intimacy, at once singular and universal. In class, unexpectedly, we were treated to a demonstration of just how broadly these small domestic moments are shared across linguistic and cultural borders.

One woman in the class, Mary Jo Marsden, a Newfoundland teacher of deaf children, signed the story in American Sign Language (ASL) while Peter read. Then Yu Ming Ye from Shanghai read it in Mandarin, and finally Karma Dyenka and Zinpai Zangmo, two women from Bhutan, read it in their native dialects of Sharshop and Dhzongka. By the end of the readings we were beginning to feel triumphantly multilingual as we distinguished some of the basic phonemes linking cultures. But a different cross-cultural connection became suddenly visible.

The mothers in the group could not help performing the actions, swinging up imaginary babies and kissing them. The two people who were not mothers read the texts without physical motion. Everyone in the class immediately picked up the difference—and the bitter irony in relation to our reading of *Bitter Milk*. Grumet's book deals with conflicts between domestic nurturing and public schooling. All the mothers, including me, were separated from young children so that we could come to university. The times varied from a few days a week (me), to a few weeks (Mary Jo), to two years (Yu Ming and Zinpai). We understood that at least one layer of our individual discomfort with the book came from the competing loyalties to our own children and to the children we teach. Nevertheless, we were able to recognize that our 'maternal' readings had been produced by the circumstances of our lives, not by the events in the

76

book. The sharp contrast between mothers and non-mothers was dramatic, but focusing on it didn't get us closer to what was transgressive. So we went on, now looking at the central scenes: the kissing of the baby's belly, toes and eyes.

Gradually the conversation turned to analogous scenes, as we asked what similar images the kissing sequences evoked. We found it impossible to look at the grandmother tasting baby toes without also seeing the grainy image of Fergie having her toes sucked by a Texan lover in the tabloid photographs that splashed around the world. An uncomfortable kind of voyeurism, this was probably inevitable in a global village created by digital (pun intended) technology. In articulating the connection between the two toe-sucking scenes we located the source of our discomfort. That's not the end of the story. Our increased sensitivity to meanings beyond the literal precipitated another kind of awareness, this time about the way culture is embedded in language.

In class we talked about how pleased we had been at being able to pick out the word 'daddy' in each rendition of *"More More More"*. In ASL I'd noticed (remembering Cixous' binary poem) that 'daddy' was a 'head' sign, thumb pointing at the forehead and fingers waving outwards. When I asked Mary Jo about this, she realized that the ASL signs for words like 'intelligence' and 'thought' were cognates of the 'daddy' sign—and that the signs linked to women and mothering were 'oral' signs. As she fitted this insight to her ASL vocabulary, gender-coded signs and words began to tumble from her mouth and hands.

Mary Jo's shocked exhilaration had a profound effect: I watched Yu Ming struggle to contain a gathering anger. She couldn't stay silent. She went to the board and drew the Chinese characters for 'papa' and 'mama' . She told us that the ideograph for 'papa' incorporates the sign for 'axe', includes the sense that it is made of metal and contains an underlying meaning that it is as valuable as gold. The implication, she explained, is that 'men are as important as gold'. Then she told us about the ideograph for 'mama', which is made up of 'woman' and 'horse', implying that mothers 'are supposed to work like

The ideograph for 'mama' [top] comprises 'woman' and 'horse'. Women belong to the home, and they are supposed to 'work like a horse'. The upper part of the ideograph for 'papa' implies the axe, though it originally meant metal and represents gold, implying that men are as important as gold.

horses'. 'Five thousand years of culture,' she added in disgust.

Like Mary Jo, Yu Ming hadn't noticed the gender coding in her language before, and she wasn't happy about this new knowledge. Their recognition scenes alerted all of us in the class to ways in which cultural values are embedded in language. Signs became readable only because we had been exploring a level of language tangential to its immediate signifying function. Later, long after the course was finished, I understood how instrumental our *"More More More"* discussion had been in alerting me to other levels of language contributing to a notice-ably changed contemporary idiom.

Learning to listen

I returned to *"More More More"*, this time thinking of it as a contact-zone text. I have borrowed 'contact zone' from Mary Louise Pratt—who borrowed it from linguistics, 'where the term contact language refers to improvised languages [like Creole and Yiddish] that develop among speakers of different native languages who need to communicate with each other consistently' (6). Vera Williams's picture book had proved to be a contact zone between private domestic and public school spaces, between security and threat, between the word and the body, between language and sign, and between parents and children.

When I asked myself what *"More More More"* reminded me of (taking my cue from a suggested 'framework' question in *Tell Me* by Aidan Chambers), two other picture books came to mind: *Peepo!* by Janet and Allan Ahlberg and *So Much* by Trish Cooke and Helen Oxenbury. As in traditional nursery verse, both texts offer intimations of loss, play threats and play fights, and both are intended for adult performance with an infant.

In *"More More More"* Little Guy 'runs away so fast', but 'Little Guy's daddy / catches that baby up all right. / He throws that baby high'. *Peepo!*, set in the England of World War Two, counterpoints the even rhythms of a baby's day (waking, eating, playing, sleeping) against jagged background threats of wartime destruction and possible loss. At the end Daddy, in his uniform, prepares to leave as the baby, in his pyjamas, prepares for bed. And in *So Much*—composed partly in contact-zone Creole harmonies—though the loving family is there, so is the intimation of threat, and the thrill of potential danger. Uncle Didi, for example, 'put the baby / on his shoulders, / and it felt shaky, shaky. / He flip-flap him over / till he nearly drop him. / "Aieeeeee!"' Later Nannie and Gran-Gran want to 'eat the baby' (shades of *Where the Wild Things Are*) and Cousin Kay-Kay and Big Cousin Ross want to 'fight the baby'.

And they wrestle
and they wrestle.
He push the baby first,
the baby hit him back.
He give the baby pinch,
the baby give him slap.
And then they laugh
and laugh and laugh.
"Huh, huh huh!"

For any student of nursery verse the juxtaposition of security and threat in *"More More More"*, *Peepo!* and *So Much* is familiar and well documented by Iona and Peter Opie in *The Oxford*

Dictionary of Nursery Rhymes. In 1951 the Opies noted that 'the overwhelming majority of nursery rhymes . . . are survivals of an adult code of joviality, and . . . by present standards, strikingly unsuitable for those of tender years' (3). Standards have changed since 1951. The vicissitudes of life, there for all to see in verses which originated in 'barrack room[s]', 'taverns' and 'mug houses' (4), don't look quite so unsuitable in a world where the sex lives of the world's major politicians are reported hourly to children and grown-ups—as news.

The Opie link leads to another transgressive book recently marketed for children: *We Are All in the Dumps with Jack and Guy*, with pictures by Maurice Sendak and text straight from the nursery canon. In *The Oxford Dictionary of Nursery Rhymes* the verse reads: 'Jack and Gye / Went out in the rye, / And they found a little boy / with one black eye' (265). To late twentieth-century ears the verse sounds chillingly modern. It sells because Sendak is a famous picture-book artist; his cachet enables an otherwise obscure traditional verse to circulate. *Lullabies, Lyrics and Gallows Songs* by the nineteenth-century poet Christian Morgenstern, in a new edition illustrated by Lisbeth Zwerger, offers another example of the presence of dangers lurking beyond the nursery. After a period in which the rough character of nursery verse was often strained out of collections destined for sale to parents for use with their children (rather than to anthropologists and folklorists), some of it is attaining a refreshed currency.

We Are All in the Dumps remains troubling to many adults who share books with children. In Sendak's haunting illustration the Trump tower looms solid and huge over the newspaper shacks of the homeless. In downtown Toronto, where I live, that image is brought to life daily by the eyes of homeless adolescents in the streets. Sendak's vision of contemporary urban life is an exact match for traditional nursery verse: the formidable and the vulnerable in stark contrast.

Once the nursery-verse connections are made explicit, a pattern, a definable characteristic of contemporary books for young children, becomes readable. Authored texts, like their traditional counterparts, can be at once joyous and dangerous, soothing in tone and threatening in subject.

Listening to baby talk

I knew that the authored texts I'd been working with, especially *So Much* and *"More More More"*, shared with nursery verse a characteristic tension between security and threat. Author and critic Marina Warner focused on the same tension in a lecture at the 1997 Modern Languages Association Conference in Toronto, previewing her new study of threatening lullabies and comic ogres, *No Go the Bogeyman: On Scaring, Lulling and Making Mock*. In it she discussed an aspect of lullaby language that I had only tangentially recognized in my study of nursery verse: its kinship with other kinds of 'infant-directed' talk.

The infant-directed talk characteristic of nursery verse, lullabies, and authored stories like *So Much* is commonly called baby talk; in the language of psycholinguistics, infant development and even ethnomusicology, baby talk is called BT or 'motherese'. Increasingly the subject of scholarly research, baby talk is recognized as a vital part of a child's language development—not something to be discouraged, as used to be the case. The interesting thing is that baby-talk language is stable across cultural, linguistic and even temporal borders. It seems to exist as a lingua franca, or what Julia Kristeva calls an 'infantile language' (278), binding generation after generation of adults talking to infants.

Among the baby-talk characteristics to be heard in *So Much* are the singsong voice and the elongation of vowels ('Yoooooo hooooo') and repetition, mimicry and special pitch. And there is what Sandra Trehub and her colleagues at the Centre for Research in Human Development at the University of Toronto (from whom I've taken much of this discussion) call the 'smiling' voice. In *So Much* the smiling voice sounds like this:

It was . . .
Auntie—
Auntie Bibba

Auntie Bibba came inside with her
arms out wide, wide, wide
and one big, big smile.

It is impossible to say these lines without sounding as though you are speaking to a baby, pitch rising and voice smiling. According to Trehub's research, the smiling voice of an adult singing to a real baby is immediately distinguishable from a voice singing with no baby present.

When I ask myself why the language of the nursery is so attractive now—both as a language in books for young children and as a subject of academic attention—I wonder if it fulfils a desire for something memorable, something performative and shared rather than solitary, something opposed to the disconnected daily assault of forgettable, transitory TV language and e-mail messages. And I'm reminded of what Ted Hughes says in another context about desire for a language able to communicate 'below the levels where differences appear' (Smith 47), a language akin to music.

Though Hughes would be horrified by the idea, I expect, a desire for a below-words level of communication might explain the huge success of BBC-TV's *Teletubbies*. In a *New York Times* article Sarah Lyall notes that *Teletubbies* is so cool that two groups of non-infants are watching it: adolescents coming home from clubs (high on ecstasy?) and members of the gay community. Lyall describes Tinky Winky as 'the first gay icon for preschool children, because of the way he cavorts with his handbag' (41). Once kids, cultural anthropologists and 'cool hunters' (people who search out street trends for commercial development) latch onto something, a change in cultural sensibilities is on the way. Baby talk is so cool, it is becoming a contact language facilitating communication across generations and cultural borderlines.

In the context of the celebrity of *Teletubbies*, the scholarly research on relationships between baby talk and language development, and Warner's work on lullabies, my readings of nursery-verse connections with authored texts for young children seem part of an emerging pattern. *"More More More"*, *So Much* and *Peepo!* begin to appear not as randomly occurring examples of contemporary nursery verse but as texts sharing a level of language that articulates a linguistic and emotional response to the conditions of our times. This language is a cognate of nursery verse and lullabies in that it

· — makes use of the stylistic features of motherese and lullabies as currently identified by socio- and psycholinguists and musicologists; these features include nursery pitch, elongation of vowels, and singsong nursery verse;
— often contains threatening or transgressive content set in soothing or lulling tones;
— is memorable in a world of forgettable language.

There will be new questions to be asked about performative forms of discourse (I have started to sketch these in 'Coming to Sing Their Being', an essay on poet Grace Nichols). In learning to attend to the music of the nursery we may not reach the top and see the whole view but we might discover how to listen to a language fraught with the suggestions of a dangerous future— lulled by the security of the voice.

RELATED READINGS *on* THINKING DIFFERENTLY

Valentine Cunningham, *In the Reading Gaol: postmodernity, texts and history*. Oxford: Blackwell, 1994.

Carol Mavor, *Pleasures Taken: Performances of Sexuality and Loss in Victorian Photographs*. Durham: Duke University Press, 1995.

Margaret Meek, *How Texts Teach What Readers Learn*. Stroud: Thimble Press, 1988.

Jane Miller, *Seductions: Studies in Reading and Culture*. London: Virago, 1990.

Marina Warner, *Managing Monsters: Six Myths of Our Time*, The Reith Lectures. London: Vintage, 1994.

MISS L. M. ALCOTT.

By Edward Salmon.

The death of Miss Louisa May Alcott on March the 6th has removed from the great republic of letters a figure familiar not only to boys and girls wherever the English language is spoken, but to readers of all ages and of more than one nationality.

It also deprives *Atalanta* of the possible privilege of printing anything from her pen. In November last the following letter was received by one of the editors in response to an invitation to write for them:—

"DEAR SIR,

"If my uncertain health permits, I shall be very glad to send you a short story by and by. I naturally take a great interest in all that concerns juvenile literature, and am happy to help in its improvement if I can. The serial is doubtful, as overwork in the past makes it unwise to promise any long effort for the future ... Should health return, I shall enjoy sending my contribution to the dear English boys and girls who have so kindly received my other books and tales. With best wishes for the success of your excellent enterprise,

"I am,
"Yours truly,
"*Louisa May Alcott*"

When Miss Alcott says that she is happy to help in the improvement of literature for the young, her words have other than a conventional meaning. The last quarter of a century has witnessed a change for the better in the character of books for boys and girls which is little short of marvellous, and to this change no one has contributed more largely than Miss Alcott.

Miss Alcott was born on November the 29th, 1833 [sic], in Germantown, Pennsylvania, of a mother noted for her beauty, and a father remarkable for his kindliness of heart and his learning. An incident, eloquent of the spirit which Miss Alcott inherited, is related of her father, who was then a humble teacher. Finding it impossible to rule his scholars by the cane, he one day threatened that the next boy who laid himself open to chastisement should take the rod and strike his master across the palm, thus reversing the order of things. Only once did he consider it necessary to carry out his threat, and then the shame which the guilty lads felt at having to strike their indulgent principal was so great that they literally went and sinned no more.[1] Anticipating the tolerance of later days, Mr. Alcott admitted coloured lads to his school, but the storm raised by this proceeding ruined his teaching prospects in Germantown, and in 1839 he moved with his family to Concord.

Here he found himself one of the brilliant set which congregated about R.W. Emerson, and Miss Alcott's early years were passed in a society likely above all else to generate a love of literature. She read the best works that came to her hand, and she has herself told us how Emerson helped her.

[1] Mr. M. D. Conway: *Emerson at Home*.

"When the book mania fell upon me at fifteen," she says, "I used to venture into Mr. Emerson's library and ask what I should read, never conscious of the audacity of my demand, so genial was my welcome. His kind hand offered to me the riches of Shakespeare, Dante, Goëthe, and Carlyle, and I gratefully recall the sweet patience with which he led me round the book-lined room, till 'the new and very interesting book' was found, and the indulgent smile he wore when I proposed something far above my comprehension. 'Wait a little for that,' he said; 'meantime try this, and if you like it, come again.' For many of these wise books I am waiting still, very patiently, because in his own I have found the truest delight and best inspiration of my life."

At eight Miss Alcott wrote a short poem, *To a Robin*, which so gratified her mother that she declared if her daughter "kept on in this hopeful way she might become a second Shakespeare in time." At sixteen Miss Alcott undertook to teach a small class of her own, and wrote a book called *Flower Fables*, which saw the light in 1855. Miss Sarah Bolton says that she improvised short stories for her pupils in place of the theological discourses to which Mr. Alcott treated them. This was the beginning of the long years of work, "fifteen of them, which should give the girl such rich, though sometimes bitter experiences, that she could write the most fascinating books from her own history. In her volume called *Work*, published when she became famous, she told many of the sorrows of her early years in those of Christie." Removing to Boston she laboured hard by day and wrote

frequently by night. At nineteen she earned her first five dollars as an author, and contributed several short stories to a Boston paper. One of these she dramatised, and but for the fact that the manager of the theatre broke his leg and their contract was annulled, Miss Alcott would probably have herself become an actress. She found sensational stories pay best at this period, and wrote with remarkable facility. A manuscript which she offered to the then editor of *The Atlantic Monthly*, Mr. J. T. Fields, was returned, with a hint that she should stick to teaching. What one cannot help regarding as Miss Alcott's opportunity came in 1861-2, when America entered upon the gigantic conflict which resulted in the overthrow of slavery in that country.

The schoolroom was replaced by the hospital ward, and the boys and girls were abandoned in the interests of the patriotic men who were fighting at once for the unity of their country and justice for the blacks. If the struggle showed the New World what its men were made of, it showed also what its women were. The "year that suddenly sang by the mouths of the round lipp'd cannon," as Walt Whitman forcibly and ruggedly puts it, was a period of crises—crises in the life of the nation, crises in the lives of individuals. It made America whole, and it gave men and women alike new and exalted ideas of the great drama in which all have to play a part. Miss Alcott was one of a body of ministering angels who tended day and night at the bedside of heroes who had fallen in the cruel crash of civil strife. Had she not been a hospital nurse, *Little Women*, and a dozen or more of her best short stories would never have been given to the world in the form they were, and might never have secured their author a place among the first writers of her time. Miss Alcott's experiences were of a very varied character; now tragic, now pathetic, now even revolting. She has recorded them in *Hospital Sketches* and other places.

"It was a strange life," she writes, "asleep half the day, exploring Washington the other half, and all night hovering, in a red rigolette, over the slumbering sons of man. I liked it, and found many things to amuse, instruct, and interest me. The snores alone were quite a study, varying from the mild sniff to the stentorian snort, which startled the echoes and hoisted the performer erect to accuse his neighbour of the deed, magnanimously forgive him, and, 'wrapping the drapery of his couch about him', lie down to vocal slumber. After listening for a week to this band of wind instruments, I indulged in the belief that I could recognize each by the snore alone. . . . I would have given much to have possessed the art of sketching, for many of the faces became wonderfully interesting when unconscious. Some grew stern and grim, the men evidently dreaming of war, as they gave orders, groaned over their wounds, or cursed the rebels vigorously; some grew sad and infinitely pathetic, as if the pain, borne silently all day, revenged itself by now betraying what the man's pride had concealed so well. Often the roughest grew young and pleasant when sleep smoothed the hard lines away, letting the real nature assert itself; many almost seemed to speak, and I learned to know these men better by night than through any intercourse by day. Sometimes they disappointed me, for faces that looked merry and good in the light seemed bad and sly when the shadows came and though they made no confidence in words I read their lives, leaving them to wonder at the change of manner this midnight magic wrought in their nurse. A few talked busily; one drummer boy sang sweetly, though no persuasions could win a note from him by day."

Weird vigils indeed they must have been! Sometimes Miss Alcott's experience was deeply touching, and in a beautiful passage which is too long to quote she related an incident of the last moments of an "earnest, brave, and faithful" man, strong, yet doomed to die of a cruel wound, the pain of which he bore with the patience of a saint.

Little Women appeared in 1868. It is a fact, I believe, that the publisher to whom the manuscript was sent placed it in the hands of his niece, a girl of sixteen, and her complete absorption in the story determined him to print it without delay. From 1868 to 1887 Miss Alcott's name occupied a prominent place every season among the authors of books for young people. A few years ago she is said to have gone into a Boston book store to give an order, when the assistant, who did not know who she was, assured her they were too busy to attend to her wishes then, as they had got to meet an urgent demand from a Western firm for an extra 20,000 copies of *Little Women*. "As soon as they got out of the store," we are told, "her companion turned to her with some congratulatory expression. 'Ah,' said Miss Alcott, drawing a long breath, 'I have waited fifteen years for this day.'" When *Little Men* appeared three years later, fifty thousand copies were ordered in advance, and from her books published during the last twenty years, Miss Bolton says, the author of *Little Women* received about 20,000*l*. The money was not lightly earned. "In her hardest working days," Mrs. Moulton declares, "she used to write fourteen hours in the twenty-four, and scarcely tasted food till her daily task was done. When she has a story to write she goes to Boston, hires a quiet room and shuts herself up in it. In a month or so the book will be done, and its author comes out 'tired, hungry, and cross,' and ready to go back to Concord and vegetate for a time."

The secret of the popularity of Miss Alcott's work is not difficult to discover. It is that she gave her own large heart to her creations—if Jo and Amy and Meg and Laurie and Mr. and Mrs. March can properly be called creations. They are rather pen and ink portraits of living beings—none other in fact than her parents and sisters and friend. Jo was to Miss Alcott what David Copperfield was to Charles Dickens. After the first few pages of *Little Women* one knows Jo personally. Her character, her sympathies, her trials, stamp her upon the memory as one worthy of a place among one's literary friends. She is a delightful girl, and none the less lovable for her boyish proclivities. "Fun for ever and no grubbage" is her motto; and directly she comes into one's presence one feels that a serious face for long is impossible. Jo's efforts to write are again, we may be sure, but the reflection of Miss Alcott's own struggles, and we get a glimpse in *Good Wives* of how it is that Miss Alcott is neither sensational nor goody-goody. "Morals don't sell," said Mr. Dashwood; and as the aspirant *littérateur* soon came

to regard sensationalism as unworthy of her, she struck the happy medium which has proved so acceptable to the little men and women on both sides of the Atlantic.

Miss Alcott's work, like Meg's "small nest," has been "eloquent of home love." Nor did she lose sight of the fact that God reigns over hearts and hearths and battle-fields alike. She makes you feel the fact without for ever reminding you of it. This accounts for the healthy effect of her books as well as for their popularity.

Miss Alcott, if one may take Jo's views as her own, was never prone to write "with a purpose." She did not claim to have a mission. None the less her mission has probably been great, and girls who have studied her can hardly have failed to acquire fresh ideas of the noble *rôle* which woman may play, and is called on to play, in life. Rose, the heroine of *Eight Cousins*, discovers when she reaches her teens that "girls are made to take care of boys." "You boys," she says, "need somebody to look after you; so I am going to do it: for girls are nice peacemakers, and know how to manage people." Miss Alcott evidently also thought that girls were the proper guardians of their brothers, and in the same way, that women were all-powerful for good in their relations with men. Meg's conduct towards her husband is an exemplification of this, and if Miss Alcott's stories serve to start young people in the world with an emphasized assurance of the truth of the view expounded by Rose, her books will have been written to a very high purpose indeed.

Works Cited

Janet & Allan Ahlberg, *Peepo!* (1981). Harmondsworth: Picture Puffin, 1983.

Janice M. Alberghene & Beverly Lyon Clark, editors, *Little Women and the Feminist Imagination*. New York: Garland, 1998.

Louisa May Alcott, *Alternative Alcott*, edited by Elaine Showalter. New Brunswick, N.J.: Rutgers University Press, 1988.

Louisa May Alcott, *The Feminist Alcott: Stories of a Woman's Power*, edited and with an introduction by Madeleine Stern. Boston: Northeastern University Press, 1996.

Louisa May Alcott, *Little Women* (1868), edited and with an introduction by Elaine Showalter. Harmondsworth: Penguin, 1989.

Louisa May Alcott, *Louisa May Alcott Unmasked: Collected Thrillers*, edited and with an introduction by Madeleine Stern. Boston: Northeastern University Press, 1995.

Hans Christian Andersen, *Hans Christian Andersen: The Complete Fairy Tales and Stories*, translated from the Danish by Erik Christian Haugaard (1974). Garden City, N.Y.: Anchor Doubleday, 1983.

Maxwell Armfield, illustrator, *Fairy Tales from Hans Andersen*, translated by Mrs E. Lucas. New York: J.M. Dent, 1910.

Edwin Arnold, poem on opening page of *Atalanta*, Vol. 1, No. 1, October 1887.

Bill Ashcroft, Gareth Griffiths & Helen Tiffin, *The Empire Writes Back: Theory and Practice in Post-Colonial Literature*. London: Routledge, 1989.

Atalanta. London: Hatchards, 1887-98.

Nina Auerbach, *Communities of Women: An Idea in Fiction*. Cambridge, Mass.: Harvard University Press, 1978.

Mikhail Bakhtin, *Rabelais and His World*, translated by H. Iswolky. Bloomington: Indiana University Press, 1984.

Nina Bawden, letter to Lissa Paul, 15 June 1993.

Nina Bawden, *Carrie's War* (1973). Harmondsworth: Puffin, 1974.

Nina Bawden, *In My Own Time: Almost an Autobiography*. London: Virago, 1994.

Nina Bawden, 'The Outside Child', *Horn Book*, November/December 1991, pages 688-94.

Nina Bawden, 'Through the Dark Wood', *Innocence & Experience: Essays & Conversations on Children's Literature* (1980). Compiled and edited by Barbara Harrison and Gregory Maguire from programs presented at Simmons College Center for the Study of Children's Literature, Boston, Massachusetts. New York: Lothrop, Lee & Shepard, 1987.

Simone de Beauvoir, *The Second Sex* (1952), translated and edited by H.M. Parshley. New York: Vintage, 1974.

Blue Beard; or Female Curiosity and Little Red Riding Hood. London: Pinnock & Maunder Mentorian Press, 1817.

Ruth Bottigheimer, *Grimms' Bad Girls and Bold Boys: The Social and Moral Vision of the Tales*. New Haven: Yale University Press, 1987.

Cleanth Brooks, *The Well Wrought Urn: Studies in the Structure of Poetry* (1947). New York: Harcourt Brace, 1956.

Peter Brooks, *Reading for the Plot: Design and Intention in Narrative*. New York: Knopf, 1984.

Anthony Browne, illustrator, *Hansel and Gretel* (1981). New York: Knopf, 1988.

Rachel Brownstein, *Becoming a Heroine: Reading about Women in Novels* (1982). Harmondsworth: Penguin, 1984.

Nancy Ekholm Burkert, illustrator, *Snow-White and the Seven Dwarfs: A Tale from the Brothers Grimm*, translated by Randall Jarrell. New York: Farrar, Straus & Giroux, 1972.

John Burningham, *John Patrick Norman McHennessy—the boy who was always late*. London: Jonathan Cape, 1987.

Joseph Campbell, *The Hero with a Thousand Faces*. Second edition. Princeton, N.J.: Princeton University Press, 1968.

The Captain: A Magazine for Boys and Old Boys, London: George Newnes, 1899-1924.

Lewis Carroll, *Through the Looking-Glass*, illustrated by John Tenniel (1872). The Macmillan Alice. London: Macmillan, 1991.

Angela Carter, *The Bloody Chamber and Other Stories* (1979). Harmondsworth: Penguin, 1981.

Angela Carter, editor, *The Virago Book of Fairy Tales*. London: Virago, 1990.

Aidan Chambers, *Tell Me: Children, Reading & Talk*. Stroud: Thimble Press, 1993.

Hélène Cixous, 'Sorties: Out and Out: Attacks / Ways Out / Forays', *The Newly Born Woman* by Hélène Cixous & Catherine Clément (1975), translated by Betsy Wing. Introduction by Sandra M. Gilbert. Theory and History of Literature, volume 24. Minneapolis: University of Minnesota Press, 1986. The lines on pages 38-9 are reprinted from the first page of the Cixous article (63).

Jill Ker Conway, *The Road from Coorain* (1989). New York: Vintage, 1990.

Trish Cooke, *So Much*, illustrated by Helen Oxenbury. London: Walker Books, 1994.

Alice Corkran, 'Chapters from the Story of My Girlhood', *The Girl's Realm* 7 (November 1904), pages 277-86.

Walter Crane, *The Bases of Design*. London: G. Bell, 1904.

Walter Crane, *Bluebeard*. Walter Crane's Toy Books. London: Routledge, 1873.

Walter Crane, *Sleeping Beauty*. Walter Crane's Toy Books. London: Routledge, 1876.

Walter Crane, illustrator, *The Child's Socialist Reader*, edited by A.A. Watts. London: Twentieth Century Press, 1907.

Valentine Cunningham, *In the Reading Gaol: postmodernity, texts and history*. Oxford: Blackwell, 1994.

Terry Eagleton, *Literary Theory: An Introduction*. Oxford: Blackwell, 1983.

Judith Fetterly, '*Little Women*: Alcott's Civil War', *Feminist Studies* 5 (Summer 1979). Reprinted in Stern, pages 140-3.

Liz Forgan, 'How was it for you, girls?' *The Observer*, 19 February 1995.

Fiona French, *Snow White in New York*. Oxford: Oxford University Press, 1986.

Sigmund Freud, 'An Autobiographical Study' 1925-34. *Sigmund Freud: Volume 15. Historical and Expository Works on Psychoanalysis.* Translated from the German under the general editorship of James Strachey. Harmondsworth: Penguin, 1993.

Northrop Frye, *Anatomy of Criticism: Four Essays*. Princeton, N.J.: Princeton University Press, 1971.

Lazlo Gal, illustrator, *Hans Christian Andersen's The Little Mermaid*, retold by Margaret Crawford Maloney. Toronto: Methuen, 1983.

Jane Gallop, *Around 1981: Academic Feminist Literary Theory*. New York: Routledge, 1992.

Sandra M. Gilbert & Susan Gubar, *The Madwoman in the Attic: The Woman Writer and the Nineteenth-Century Literary Imagination*. New Haven: Yale University Press, 1979.

Carol Gilligan, *In a Different Voice: Psychological Theory and Women's Development*. Cambridge, Mass.: Harvard University Press, 1982.

The Girl's Realm. London: S. H. Bousfield & Co, 1898-1915.

Gerald Graff, *Professing Literature: An Institutional History*. Chicago: University of Chicago Press, 1987.

Stephen Greenblatt & Giles Gunn, editors, *Redrawing the Boundaries: The Transformation of English and American Literary Studies*. New York: Modern Languages Association of America, 1992.

Jacob Grimm & Wilhelm Grimm, *The Complete Fairy Tales of the Brothers Grimm*, 2 volumes (1812, 1815). Translated and with an introduction by Jack Zipes. New York: Bantam Books, 1988.

Lawrence Grossberg, Cary Nelson & Paula Treichler, editors, *Cultural Studies*. New York: Routledge, 1992.

Madeline Grumet, *Bitter Milk: Women and Teaching*. Amherst: University of Massachusetts Press, 1988.

David Grylls, *Guardians and Angels: Parents and Children in Nineteenth-Century Literature*. London: Faber, 1978.

Hansel and Gretel: An Appalachian Version. Directed by Tom Davenport, 1975.

N. Katherine Hayles, *Chaos Bound: Orderly Disorder in Contemporary Literature and Science*. Ithaca, N.Y.: Cornell University Press, 1990.

Carolyn Heilbrun, *Reinventing Womanhood*. New York: Norton, 1979.

Norman Holland, *5 Readers Reading*. New Haven: Yale University Press, 1975.

Ted Hughes, letter to Lissa Paul, 1 May 1984.

Peter Hunt, editor, *Criticism, Theory and Children's Literature*. Oxford: Blackwell, 1991.

Peter Hunt, editor, *The International Companion Encyclopedia of Children's Literature*. London: Routledge, 1996.

Trina Schart Hyman, illustrator, *Rapunzel*. Retold from the Grimm by Barbara Rogasky. New York: Holiday House, 1982.

Wolfgang Iser, *The Act of Reading: A Theory of Aesthetic Response*. Baltimore: Johns Hopkins University Press, 1978.

Elizabeth Janeway, *New York Times Book Review*, 29 September 1968. Reprinted in Stern, page 97.

Elizabeth Lennox Keyser, *Whispers in the Dark: The Fiction of Louisa May Alcott*. Knoxville: University of Tennessee Press, 1993.

Annette Kolodny, 'A Map for Rereading: Gender and Interpretation of Literary Texts'. *The New Literary History*, 1980, reprinted in *The New Feminist Criticism: Essays on Women, Literature & Theory*, edited by Elaine Showalter. New York: Pantheon, 1985.

Julia Kristeva, *Desire in Language: A Semiotic Approach to Literature and Art*, translated by Thomas Gora, Alice Jardine & Leon S. Roudiez. New York: Columbia University Press, 1980.

Susan Laird, 'The Ideal of the Educated Teacher: "Reclaiming a Conversation" with Louisa May Alcott'. *Curriculum Inquiry*, 21 3, Fall 1991, pages 271-93.

David Lodge, editor, *20th Century Literary Criticism: A Reader*. London: Longman, 1972.

Sarah Lyall, 'Tubbies say, "Eh-oh". Parents Say, "Uh-Oh".' *The New York Times*, 11 January 1998, page 41.

Margaret Mahy, *The Changeover: A Supernatural Romance*. London: Dent, 1984.

Jane Marcus, 'Alibis and Legends: The Ethics of Elsewhereness, Gender and Estrangement', *Women's Writing in Exile*, edited by Mary Lynn Broe & Angela Ingram. Chapel Hill: University of North Carolina Press, 1989, pages 269-94.

Jane Roland Martin, *Reclaiming a Conversation: The Ideal of the Educated Woman*. New Haven: Yale University Press, 1985.

Karl Marx, *Selected Writings*, edited by David McLellan. Oxford: Oxford University Press, 1977.

Maternal Literacies Group (Frankie Blake, Maria Christine, Winifred Fulton, Peter Gorham, Marilyn Graham, Janet Kershaw, Midge Leavitt, Pam Nason & Lissa Paul), 'The Pig's Tale', *Primary Teaching Studies 9*, University of North London, Summer 1996, pages 2-9.

Carol Mavor, *Pleasures Taken: Performances of Sexuality and Loss in Victorian Photographs*. Durham: Duke University Press, 1995.

Margaret Meek, *How Texts Teach What Readers Learn*. Stroud: Thimble Press, 1988.

Jane Miller, *Seductions: Studies in Reading and Culture*. London: Virago, 1990.

Toril Moi, *Sexual/Textual Politics: Feminist Literary Theory*. New Accents. London: Methuen, 1985.

Christian Morgenstern, *Lullabies, Lyrics and Gallows Songs*, translated by Anthea Bell, selected and illustrated by Lisbeth Zwerger. London: North-South, 1995.

Mitzi Myers, 'Romancing the Moral Tale: Maria Edgeworth and the Problematics of Pedagogy', *Romanticism and Children's Literature in Nineteenth-Century England*, edited by James Holt McGavran. Athens, Georgia: University of Georgia Press, 1991, pages 96-128.

Grace Nichols, *The Fat Black Woman's Poems*. London: Virago, 1984.

Grace Nichols, compiler, *Poetry Jump-up: A Collection of Black Poetry* (1988). Harmondsworth: Puffin, 1990.

One Week in March: a survey of the literature pupils read. London: Schools Curriculum and Assessment Authority, 1995.

Iona & Peter Opie, editors, *The Oxford Dictionary of Nursery Rhymes* (1951). Oxford: Oxford University Press, 1997.

Mechthild Papousek & Hanus Papousek, 'The Meanings of Melodies in Motherese in Tone and Stress Languages', *Infant Behaviour and Development* 14 (1991), pages 415-40.

Coventry Patmore, 'The Wife's Tragedy', *The Angel in the House* Part 1. London: John W. Parker, 1854.

Lissa Paul, 'Coming to Sing Their Being', *Girls, Boys, Books, Toys: Gender, Culture, Children's Literature*, edited by Margaret Higonnet & Beverly Lyon Clark. In preparation. Baltimore: Johns Hopkins University Press, 1999.

Lissa Paul, 'Enigma Variations: What Feminist Theory Knows about Children's Literature', *Signal*, September 1987, pages 186-202.

Lissa Paul, 'Feminist Criticism: From Sex-Role Stereotyping to Subjectivity', *The International Companion Encyclopedia of Children's Literature*, edited by Peter Hunt. London: Routledge, 1996.

Charles Perrault, *The Fairy Tales of Charles Perrault* (1697), translated by Angela Carter, illustrated by Martin Ware. London: Gollancz, 1977.

Beatrix Potter, *The Tale of Peter Rabbit* (1902). London: Warne, 1987.

Mary Louise Pratt, *Imperial Eyes: Travel Writing and Transculturation*. London: Routledge, 1992.

John Crowe Ransom, *The New Criticism*. Norfolk, Conn.: New Directions, 1941.

Adrienne Rich, *Of Woman Born: Motherhood as Experience and Institution*. New York: Norton, 1976.

Adrienne Rich, 'Women and Honor: Some Notes on Lying' (1975). *On Lies, Secrets and Silence: Selected Prose 1966-1978*. New York: Norton, 1979.

I.A. Richards, *Practical Criticism: A Study of Literary Judgement* (1929). New York: Harcourt, 1960.

Christopher Ricks & Leonard Michaels, editors, *The State of the Language*. London: Faber, 1990.

Christina Rossetti, *Goblin Market*, illustrated by Martin Ware (1980). London: Gollancz Children's Paperbacks, 1989.

Leona Rostenberg, *Papers of the Bibliographical Society of America* (2nd Quarter 1943), pages 131-40. Reprinted in Stern, 43-50.

Edward Salmon, Obituary: 'Miss L. Alcott'. *Atalanta*, May 1888, pages 447-9.

Maurice Sendak, *In the Night Kitchen* (1970). New York: Trophy, 1985.

Maurice Sendak, *We Are All in the Dumps with Jack and Guy: Two Nursery Rhymes*. New York: HarperCollins, 1993.

Anne Sexton, *Transformations*, illustrated by Barbara Swan. Boston: Houghton Mifflin, 1971.

Elaine Showalter, *Hystories: Hysterical Epidemics and Modern Media*. New York: Columbia University Press, 1997.

A.C.H. Smith, *Orghast at Persepolis*. London: Methuen, 1982.

Peter Stallybrass & Allon White, *The Politics and Poetics of Transgression*. Ithaca, N.Y.: Cornell University Press, 1986.

Carolyn Steedman. *The Tidy House: Little Girls Writing*. London: Virago, 1982.

Gloria Steinem, 'How was it for you, girls?' *The Observer,* 19 February 1995.

Madeleine B. Stern. *Critical Essays on Louisa May Alcott.* Boston: G.K. Hall, 1984.

Barbara Swan. See Anne Sexton.

Tales from the Thousand and One Nights, translated and with an introduction by N.J. Dawood. Harmondsworth:Penguin, 1973.

Janet Todd, *Feminist Literary History: A Defence.* Cambridge: Polity in association with B. Blackwell, 1988.

Jane Tompkins, 'Me and My Shadow'. In Warhol & Herndl, pages 1079-92.

Sandra Trehub, Anna M. Unyk & Laurel J. Trainor, 'Adults Identify Infant-directed Music Across Cultures' (pages 193-211), 'Maternal Singing in Cross-Cultural Perspective' (pages 285-95), *Infant Behaviour and Development* 16 (1993).

Roberta Seelinger Trites, *Waking Sleeping Beauty: Feminist Voices in Children's Novels.* Iowa City: University of Iowa Press, 1997.

Edward Wagenknecht, '*Little Women* and the Domestic Sentimentalists', *Cavalcade of the American Novel from the Birth of the Nation to the Middle of the Twentieth Century* (1952). Reprinted in Stern, page 97.

Robyn Warhol & Diane Price Herndl, editors, *Feminisms: An Anthology of Literary Theory and Criticism.* New Brunswick, N.J.: Rutgers University Press, 1991.

Martin Ware. See Charles Perrault, Christina Rossetti.

Marina Warner, *From the Beast to the Blonde: On Fairy Tales and Their Tellers.* London: Chatto & Windus, 1994.

Marina Warner, *Managing Monsters: Six Myths of Our Time.* The Reith Lectures. London: Vintage, 1994.

Marina Warner, *No Go the Bogeyman: On Scaring, Lulling and Making Mock.* London: Chatto & Windus, 1998.

Vera B. Williams, *"More More More," Said the Baby: 3 Love Stories* (1990). New York: Mulberry, 1996.

W.K. Wimsatt & Monroe C. Beardsley, 'The Affective Fallacy' (1949), in Wimsatt, *The Verbal Icon: Studies in the Meaning of Poetry.* Lexington: University of Kentucky Press, 1954. Reprinted in Lodge, 348-58.

Tim Wynne-Jones, *The Maestro.* Toronto: Douglas & McIntyre, 1995.

Jack Zipes, *Don't Bet on the Prince: Contemporary Feminist Fairy Tales in North America and England.* New York: Methuen, 1986.

Jack Zipes, *Fairy Tales and the Art of Subversion: The Classical Genre for Children and the Process of Civilization.* New York: Wildman Press, 1983.

Jack Zipes, *Happily Ever After: Fairy Tales, Children and the Culture Industry.* London: Routledge, 1997.

Jack Zipes, *The Trials and Tribulations of Little Red Riding Hood: Versions of the Tale in Sociocultural Context.* South Hadley, Mass.: Bergin & Garvey, 1983.

Index

Act of Reading, 14
Affective Fallacy, 14
Ahlberg, Janet & Allan, 79
Alcott, Bronson, 50-1
Alcott, Louisa May, 41-55
Alice Through the Looking-Glass,
　*73
Alternative Alcott, 52
Anatomy of Criticism, 8
Andersen, Hans Christian, 20,
　24
Aristotle, 14
Armfield, Maxwell, 20
Arnold, Edwin, 45
Atalanta, 41, 45, 46
Auerbach, Nina, 52-3

Bakhtin, Mikhail, 65
Barnard, A.M. (pseudonym
　Louisa May Alcott), 48, 51
Bases of Design, 8
Bawden, Nina, 56-72
Beardsley, Monroe, 14
Beauvoir, Simone de, 9
Behind a Mask, 52
Beowulf, 13
Bitter Milk, 75, 76
Bleich, David, 14
'Bluebeard', 24, 25-31, 36
Brooks, Cleanth, 12
Brooks, Peter, 14
Browne, Anthony, 32, 34-36
Browning, Elizabeth Barrett, 47
Burkert, Nancy Ekholm, 36
Burningham, John, 7

Campbell, Joseph, 8

Captain, The, 46
Carrie's War, 56-72
Carter, Angela, 29-31
Chambers, Aidan, 79
Children's Literature Association
　Phoenix Award, 56
Child's Socialist Reader, 27
'Cinderella', 24
Cixous, Hélène, 15, 38-9, 77
Communities of Women, 52
Cooke, Trish, 79
Corkran, Alice, 47
Crane, Walter, 8-10, 25-31, 60

Davenport, Tom, 32
Disney, Walt, 8, 25, 37, 39
Dyenka, Karma, 76

Edgeworth, Maria, 17
Eight Cousins, 44
Eliot, T.S., 13
Emerson, Ralph Waldo, 41

Fetterly, Judith, 52
Forgan, Liz, 54
Four Quartets, 13
French, Fiona, 36, 37
Freud, Sigmund, 26, 33
From the Beast to the Blonde, 29,
　33
Frye, Northrop, 8

Gal, Laszlo, 38
Gallop, Jane, 15
Gilbert, Sandra, 15, 37, 48
Gilligan, Carol, 60, 61
Girl's Realm, 47

Goblin Market, 28
Gorham, Peter, 74-5
Greenblatt, Stephen, 13
Grimm, Jacob & Wilhelm, 23, 24, 32, 33
Grumet, Madeline, 75, 76
Grylls, David, 23
Guardians and Angels, 23
Gubar, Susan, 15, 37, 48
Gunn, Giles, 13

'Hansel and Gretel', 24, 31-6
Hayles, N. Katherine, 11-12
Heilbrun, Carolyn, 15, 52, 70
Hemingway, Ernest, 17
Henty, G.A., 46
Hero with a Thousand Faces, 8
Holland, Norman, 14
Hospital Sketches, 42
Hughes, Ted, 13-15, 82
Hyman, Trina Schart, 24

Imperial Eyes, 74
In a Different Voice, 60, 61
In My Own Time: Almost an Autobiography, 59
In the Night Kitchen, 10
Iser, Wolfgang, 14

Janeway, Elizabeth, 40, 51, 52
Jarrell, Randall, 36
John Patrick Norman McHennesy, 7
Joyce, James, 17

Keyser, Elizabeth, 52
Kinder- und Hausmärchen, 23, 33
Kolodny, Annette, 15
Kristeva, Julia, 81

Laird, Susan, 53

'Little Mermaid', 9, 20, 24, 25, 37
Little Women, 40-55, 56
Louisa May Alcott Unmasked, 52
Lullabies, Lyrics and Gallows Songs, 80
Lyall, Sarah, 82

Madwoman in the Attic, 37
Marcus, Jane, 15
Mark, Jan, 58
Marsden, Mary Jo, 76-7
Martin, Jane Roland, 62
Micmac-Maliseet Institute, 17-20
Modern Language Association *International Bibliography*, 50
Moi, Toril, 15
"More More More," Said the Baby: 3 Love Stories, 74-9, 81, 83
Morgenstern, Christian, 80
Myers, Mitzi, 17

Nesbit, E., 58
New Criticism, 12-14, 51
Newly Born Woman, 38
Nichols, Grace, 83
No Go the Bogeyman: On Scaring, Lulling and Making Mock, 81

One Week in March, 56
Opie, Iona & Peter, 79
Osborne Collection of Early Children's Books, 23, 24, 30
Outside Child, 59
Oxenbury, Helen, 79
Oxford Dictionary of Nursery Rhymes, 79-80

Patmore, Coventry, 42-3
Peepo!, 79, 83

Perrault, Charles, 24, 25, 29
Peter Rabbit, 10
Plato, 14
Plots and Counterplots, 52
Politics and Poetics of Transgression, 22
Pratt, Mary Louise, 74, 78
'Puss in Boots', 24

Ransom, John Crowe, 12, 51
'Rapunzel', 24
Redrawing the Boundaries, 13
Rich, Adrienne, 31
Richards, I.A., 12
Rossetti, Christina, 28
Rostenberg, Leona, 51

Salmon, Edward, 41-4, 47-50
Second Sex, 9
Sendak, Maurice, 10, 80
Sexton, Anne, 36, 37
Showalter, Elaine, 15, 52
Simon, Roger, 20
'Sleeping Beauty', 8-10, 23, 24, 25, 27, 60, 70
'Snow White', 8, 24, 27, 36-7, 70
Snow White in New York, 36
So Much, 79, 81, 83
Stallybrass, Peter, 17, 22, 34
Stead, Christina, 17
'Steadfast Tin Soldier', 24
Steedman, Carolyn, 44
Steinem, Gloria, 54
Stern, Madeleine, 52
Swan, Barbara, 36, 37

Tales from the Thousand and One Nights, 30
Taming of the Shrew, 9
Teletubbies, 82

Tell Me, 79
Tidy House, 44
Todd, Janet, 15
Tompkins, Jane, 15
Trehub, Sandra, 81, 82
Trites, Roberta Seelinger, 10

Verbal Icon, 12

Wagenknecht, Edward, 51
Ware, Martin, 25, 28, 29, 31, 36
Warner, Marina, 24, 29, 33, 81, 82
Warner, Sylvia Townsend, 17
Warren, Robert Penn, 51
We Are All in the Dumps with Jack and Guy, 80
Well Wrought Urn, 12
Where the Wild Things Are, 79
White, Allon, 22
Williams, Vera B., 74, 78
Wimsatt, W.K., 12, 14

Ye, Yu Ming, 76, 77-8

Zangmo, Zinpai, 76
Zipes, Jack, 24
Zwerger, Lisbeth, 80